Lessons in Poetry

For a Wayward Child of Sad Eyes and Lonely Heart

Anita Garman and John Knowlton

BALBOA
PRESS

A DIVISION OF HAY HOUSE

Copyright © 2018 Anita Garman and John Knowlton.

All rights reserved. No part of this book may be used or reproduced by any means, graphic, electronic, or mechanical, including photocopying, recording, taping or by any information storage retrieval system without the written permission of the author except in the case of brief quotations embodied in critical articles and reviews.

Balboa Press books may be ordered through booksellers or by contacting:

Balboa Press
A Division of Hay House
1663 Liberty Drive
Bloomington, IN 47403
www.balboapress.com
1 (877) 407-4847

Because of the dynamic nature of the Internet, any web addresses or links contained in this book may have changed since publication and may no longer be valid. The views expressed in this work are solely those of the author and do not necessarily reflect the views of the publisher, and the publisher hereby disclaims any responsibility for them.

The author of this book does not dispense medical advice or prescribe the use of any technique as a form of treatment for physical, emotional, or medical problems without the advice of a physician, either directly or indirectly. The intent of the author is only to offer information of a general nature to help you in your quest for emotional and spiritual well-being. In the event you use any of the information in this book for yourself, which is your constitutional right, the author and the publisher assume no responsibility for your actions.

Any people depicted in stock imagery provided by Getty Images are models, and such images are being used for illustrative purposes only. Certain stock imagery © Getty Images.

Print information available on the last page.

ISBN: 978-1-9822-0099-2 (sc)
ISBN: 978-1-9822-0098-5 (hc)
ISBN: 978-1-9822-0100-5 (e)

Library of Congress Control Number: 2018903516

Balboa Press rev. date: 04/13/2018

Contents

Acknowledgments ix
Preface xi
Introduction xvii

Chapter 1 1
Chapter 2 10
Chapter 3 19
Chapter 4 29
Chapter 5 45
Chapter 6 59
Chapter 7 82
Chapter 8 102
Chapter 9 114
Chapter 10 132
Chapter 11 145
Chapter 12 156

Epilogue 171

This book is lovingly dedicated to our family.

Sean and Amy

Tiffany, Taylor, and Luke

Acknowledgments

The wise women in my life:

Janet Falgout, PhD, who has shown me the way, step by step, through this difficult journey and the maze of my psyche with understanding, insight, and patience.

Hilary Bee, who revealed to me the beauty of my personal myth and articulated the greater meaning of my relationship with my beloved.

Carolyn Kelley Williams, who, through her insightful guidance in the Progoff way, has shown me new paths to a deeper connection with self and spirit.

The psychic medium:

Jamie Clark, who opened the door to my contact with the world of spirit and offered wise counsel on navigating that landscape.

"Neva," who loved and supported me from the very beginning of this journey and shared her remarkable gifts with me as a conduit for Johnny's messages.

The artist:

Sheila Green, who created the magical cover for the book.

My dear friends who encouraged me to write this book:

Priscilla Chomina-Botts
Karen Fogarty
Jackie Kalinsky
Rachel McDonald
Kat Rogers
Ellen Worle

Preface

I have felt from the beginning that this work was a collaborative effort between my husband and me, even though he moved on from this life long before the book was begun. His poems appear throughout, and all but a small portion of the epilogue is composed of the recollections that he wrote in later years. I have felt his guiding spirit throughout the writing of this book.

Your task is not to seek for love, but merely to seek and find all the barriers within yourself that you have built against it.
Rumi

Lovers don't finally meet
somewhere.
They're in each other all
along.
Rumi

Invocation

I invoke you
Oh, my Muse
Of Truth and Beauty,
Let only words
Of light and poetry,
Joy and harmony
Flow from my pen,
Widening soul ways
For your constant presence.

Prince of Poetry,
Bringer of magic,
Cause words to bloom
Beneath your touch
Within my mind,
Spring from my hand
As it were your own.
And may your lessons ever
Be anchored in my heart.

Introduction

In my memory, Mrs. Hagen is an old lady. She wore her white hair in a bun, and her dresses came almost to her ankles, just above her black, laced shoes. My family lived next door to her in 1937, when I was three, and one of my earliest memories is reaching my tiny hand through the chicken wire fence that separated our properties to snitch her plump raspberries, pull them from the vine, and pop them into my mouth. I was never quite sure if this was permitted or not, but I was never reprimanded.

Later, when I had grown taller and my mother and I had moved across the street to live with my grandmother as my father went his separate way, Mrs. Hagen invited me into her cellar. It was accessed by a wooden door that lay almost at ground level, which she would pull upward to reveal the stairs leading down into the dark, pungent earth. In the cellar, which seemed to be full of potatoes lying about on tables, she showed me how to pull the white sprouts from the potatoes, an activity that I delighted in, so much so that I asked her repeatedly throughout the year if it was yet time to do the potatoes. She would shake her head kindly, saying, "Not quite."

When I was seven, she gave me a small book entitled *Rumpty Dudget's Tower*,[1] which I read repeatedly through the next two years. On the cover was a dwarf-sized man with a gray beard reaching to

---

[1] Julian Hawthorne, *Rumpty Dudget's Tower* (New York: Frederick Stokes Company, 1928.) Julian Hawthorne was the son of novelist Nathaniel Hawthorne and Sophia Peabody Hawthorne.

his knees, wearing a gray cape that dragged on the ground and a tall, gray, broad-brimmed hat. Behind him, on a hill among the trees, rose a towering castle with many turrets. It was easy for me to identify with the princess Hilda, the heroine of the story whose mother was away in a distant country. My own mother during this time had been taken to a tuberculosis sanitarium for an indefinite period. In the mother's absence, Hilda and her two younger brothers were watched over by a huge cat with glowing eyes. They lived in "the most beautiful palace ever built" and played daily in "a garden that was the loveliest ever seen.' But only a hedge separated their garden from the property of Rumpty Dudget, an evil little man who snatched children to put in the corners of his tower. He had only one corner left to fill, and when that happened, he would be master of the whole country, causing the children's palace to disappear and the garden to turn to stones and brambles.

Of course, the inevitable happened, and one of Hilda's brothers was snatched and placed in the last empty corner of the tower. Everything was lost. Yet Hilda was offered redemption, but only if she could perform three seemingly impossible tasks, which involved journeys to the lower and upper kingdoms. The rest of the story was a long tale of the vicissitudes of her journey, but she was at last victorious; the children were freed, the garden was restored, the mother returned, and they all lived happily ever after. It was a most delightfully told fairy tale.

My grandmother had a small house on a huge lot that had a wide green lawn and a variety of plants and flowers, from tall hollyhocks to squat succulents we called "hens and chickens." There was rhubarb growing along one fence, a strawberry patch in the corner, and, out front, a climbing tree. It was easy for me, playing in this lovely yard daily, to imagine myself as the princess Hilda and the rambling old stone house on the hill above the yard as Rumpty Dudget's castle.

All too soon, my idyllic childhood was disrupted by my grandmother's illness and death. I was sent to live with a minister, recommended by a distant relative, just before I entered sixth grade. I was uprooted so quickly that I had no chance to retrieve my cherished possessions, and *Rumpty Dudget's Tower* was left behind. I stayed with my new family until I graduated from high school and returned to live with my mother, who, after years in the sanitarium, had moved to another city after being cured of tuberculosis.

After my first year in college, during the summer, my mother and I returned to Bend and visited the site of my grandmother's garden. The house had been demolished. There was only a small hole in the ground that had been a cellar, accessed by a trapdoor under a rug in the living room. All the rest was brown weeds grown thigh high. Even the white picket fence was gone. All that remained was the climbing tree, which had grown to twice its height. It seemed that Rumpty Dudget had prevailed.

Chapter 1

Poetry we shared from the beginning. I was a college freshman, naïve and full of drama. He was a returning veteran, deep and melancholy. We met in French class. We dated. I recited Poe to him; he read to me Keats and Browning. And we shared other poems, ones we had written, ones we had not. To say that we were orphans is not in the realm of fact but of metaphor. We were abandoned souls who saw mirrored in each other our own lonely hearts.

I had discovered poetry when my sixth-grade teacher asked everyone in the class to memorize two poems, a moment that sparked a fascination that became a part of me. But I found no one who loved poetry, who loved the written word in the way I did, until I met him. He took me seriously, as no one ever had. And in him I found a kindred spirit.

And there was another world for me as well—the ancient world of the Middle East: Baghdad, Persian gardens, Arabian deserts, and *The Rubaiyat of Omar Khayyam*.[2] What little of this came into my consciousness, I captured and drew to my heart. He too had been allured by that world but by a different route. He had first been led to his major, Spanish literature, by reading Washington Irving's *Tales of the Alhambra*, which recounted the legends of that ancient Moorish castle. We shared our finds with each other. It was not

---

[2] Translations by Edward Fitzgerald, *The Rubaiyat of Omar Khayyam* (Garden City, New York: Doubleday & Company, Inc., 1952), 46. First printings appeared in 1858.

unlikely that we began to build a fantasy between us of lives lived together in those ancient lands.

One day in the autumn that we met, we drove to the country. He stopped the car and invited me to walk with him along a golden hillside. The grass was short and had turned with the coming of winter. After a time, he stopped and set down the sack he was carrying. He asked me to turn away and look at the view for a few minutes. This was the first surprise he ever prepared for me. I turned back to find he had spread a cloth on the ground and placed on it a baguette, a bottle of wine, and a little book that he often carried with him, *A Pocketbook of Verse*. I recognized the context immediately—a verse from *The Rubaiyat*.

> Here with a Loaf of Bread beneath the Bough,
> A Flask of Wine, a Book of Verse—and Thou
> Beside me singing in the Wilderness—
> And Wilderness is Paradise enow.

And then, when he graduated two and a half years ahead of me, he left me for his other love—the Lady Spain. Letters flew for fifteen months. When he returned, we married. In graduate school, he became enchanted with the Spanish poet Federico Garcia Lorca, born in Andalusia, where ancient Moorish influence is embedded in the culture. Ultimately, as a professor of Spanish literature, he taught the poetry of Lorca.

We built a home in the desert overlooking the city of Phoenix, brought tiles and woodwork from Mexico, including lion statuary and fountains. He named it Casa de Leones. A friend called it, in fun, the Little Alhambra. The house was always a magical place for us. We raised one child and many cats there. Our son, Sean, was born in 1968. We brought him home in the midst of a flu epidemic and anguished through his siege with a bad cold. Johnny taught him to swim by the time he was two and had to convince him the water was not dangerous when he was three. As he grew, we cheered him through seasons of Little League, swim team, and bicycle motocross. All too soon, he was tossing a mortarboard into the air and leaping from the stage.

And through the years, Johnny brought me constant gifts—flowers and his poems. And he gave his students the gift of poetry as well, made it come alive for them with his energy and passion. He championed poetry performance, often presenting Lorca's poetry in a darkened room, rising from behind a lone candle, cloaked in blackness, his face whitened as the moon, reciting in hoarsely whispered tones, "Luna, Luna, Luna."

He designed elaborate surprises for my birthdays, so that I would wake to mariachis singing from the bedroom patio or, unsuspecting, walk into a room to find my sister from Oregon had surreptitiously been transported there. One year, I planned to invite our friends in and spend a birthday at home. One by one, I called them and grew more disappointed as each apologetically told me of other plans. He immediately suggested that we go to dinner at a favorite restaurant on my birthday. That night, the hostess led us through a crowded room to a quiet alcove and started to seat us at a table filled with people. I turned to protest when a familiar face caught my eye—it was one of the friends I had invited for my birthday. I was stunned, confused, trying to figure what to make of it. And then I looked again, and the person sitting next to him was another friend I had asked to come. As the blur of faces around the table came into focus, one by one, I recognized each of those I had asked in for my birthday, who were, in my mind, scattered throughout the city, and some as far away as New Mexico. I stood in silence, trying to absorb what had happened, until at last I began to laugh. My reality, for those few seconds, was skewed to the point that I could not believe my own eyes. It was an amazing experience he had created for me.

And so, in our home on the slopes of the mountain, the years rolled by. He commissioned a mural for a wall of the living room—a unicorn with sparkling mane arriving to drink from waters inhabited by long-legged birds, which he loved. That room was the center of innumerable celebrations—the burning of the yule log as he and I danced for our guests to a medieval tune, wearing crowns of lighted candles; the weaving of garlands of oleander for the maypole dance held in the garden above the pool. Guest musicians were welcomed. Neighborhood get-togethers and, of course, special gatherings for his students were held there.

Throughout our lives, Spain was always the other woman, the language, the poetry that drew him away from me: for sabbaticals, for summer sessions abroad, for interviews with Spanish poets. These times apart were wrenchingly lonely for both of us. He wrote me of long nights in austere hotel rooms. I suffered with a deep homesickness, counting the days to his return; he was always my true home, and I his. On his return, he told me of his adventures. After months of interviewing poets in Spain, he excitedly recounted his time spent with Vicente Aleixandre, who had not yet won the Nobel Prize for Spanish literature. Seated in his study, unchanged for forty years, Aleixandre, pointing to various spots, had told Johnny, "I remember a night when Dali sat there, Luis Bunuel was over there, and Lorca here." Chills rippled along his spine, he told me, as if he felt the presence of Lorca in the room.

And there were times when I left home to lead weekend seminars or spend time in Washington visiting my father. On returning and stepping off the plane's ramp, searching for his face, happiness swelled in my chest as I ran to meet him. At home, there would be a sign on the door—Welcome Home, Anita—spelled out in flowers. Or inside, on the kitchen counter, a card, telling of his loneliness and how he looked forward to my return. Our reunions were always joyful.

My greatest regret in life is that I did not continue my own studies in Spanish, which I dropped before I had a grasp of the language. What I had learned faded quickly. It caused me to be a spectator rather than a participant in a significant part of his life. I knew, without knowledge of the language, I could never understand as he did the culture of the Spanish people or develop the love for it that he held. Spanish poetry, especially Lorca's poetry, was his religion, the thing that moved him most deeply.

He took our son and me to Granada to visit the Alhambra. There were not the crowds then that today wait outside for admittance in long queues and are allowed only half an hour within the palace. We were able to wander at will throughout the grounds. The time we spent in the Alhambra was magical. We stayed on a narrow street in an inn with a geranium-filled patio, where guitars played nightly. I experienced the feeling he had for Spain in the majesty of the castle, the fire of flamenco dancers, the wailing notes of gypsy guitars. As we walked together in the gardens of the Generalife, past cooling fountains, lily ponds, and lovely arching pavilions, we shared our fantasies of those ancient times—visions of a shadowy figure behind the lattice work, a sheikh strolling in the garden to the sound of a zither's strings. There he shared with me the experience of his first time in that city twenty-seven years before. The *Tales of the Alhambra* had led him there, and he stayed in an inn, called after the author, directly across from the palace. As he spent time within the walls of the gardens, he struck up an acquaintance with a caretaker, who was good enough to allow him to stay after hours one evening and roam the gardens alone after dark. Breathing in the magnolia-scented air, he turned his eyes upward to glimpse a light moving along the arched windows in the tower—whether candle or lantern, he couldn't tell. When the caretaker unlocked the gate for him to leave, he asked who was carrying the light in the tower. The caretaker replied, "Nadie, solamente tu y yo estamos en este lugar." ("No one. You and I are the only living souls within these walls.")

Wherever our lives took us—whether we were apart a month, a week, or only a day—coming home to each other was a special moment. Even at the end of a long evening with friends, we took time to savor each other's company before retiring. What he shared with me in those times was not the ordinary but small discoveries, the things that delighted him—an unfamiliar word he had come across in his studies. I remember particularly "palimpsest," which to him seemed magical. He explained that it was used originally to describe a manuscript that had been erased and written over so that the precious parchment could be reused, yet traces of the original writing remained, seeming to bleed through. Now "palimpsest" had broadened to become a rich metaphor describing meanings glimmering from beneath the surface.

Another time, it might be something that revealed the mystery of the natural world. He brought home one evening, from a tree on campus, a large seed pod, something I had never seen—a bit like a pine cone in shape and plainness in color. He told me it had come from the center of a magnolia blossom. Later—a day, maybe two—he exclaimed, "Look!" as he drew forth, as if by sleight of hand, the seed pod, no longer dull and unremarkable but transformed, bursting with a cascade of brilliant red, plump seeds, each clinging to a gossamer strand, having shot from the pod overnight and now hanging from its source like a ruby on a delicate thread. I delighted at such sudden beauty. He was constantly pulling aside the drab curtain of everyday life to reveal the wonder within it.

That view of the world is illustrated in a vignette he wrote in later years called "The Agate," which describes the magic he found in a simple chance meeting.[3]

He continued to find magic in the ordinary, and kindness was evident everywhere in his life. He always had a compliment for the bank or grocery store clerk, commenting on her sparkly earrings or the color of her dress. Although, early on, when he told a fellow teacher she looked like a gypsy, she didn't realize he meant it as a compliment.

During his years at ASU, he read papers in the Memorial Union featuring Spanish poets and had even gone so far afield as to present an interpretation of *Rocky Horror Picture Show*. At retirement, he gave his final presentation. The hall in the Union was crowded with students and faculty as he reviewed, with pathos and humor, the

---

[3] See the epilogue for the text of this story.

memories of his time teaching there. And then, with a smile, a nod, and a wave of his black umbrella, he did a slow dance step around the point of the umbrella, tucked it beneath his arm, and waltzed from the room in true gypsy fashion, to a roar of appreciation from his audience.

The first ten years of his retirement we filled with friends and activity. Sean would bring our granddaughter Tiffany to spend long afternoons with us, as the three of us acted out scenes from *Harry Potter*. Later, her sister, Taylor, came too. One Easter morning, after Sean and Amy had blended their families to give the girls a big brother, Luke, Johnny rented a bunny costume and delivered Easter baskets to the three of them. He liked the identity of the costume so much that he spent the rest of the day in the flower gardens along Baseline Road waving to passing motorists. We spent many summers in the Arizona mountains taking daylong hikes and watching squirrels from the balcony of our condo. The first year there, we took our cat, Serendipity. The second year, Annie cat was added, and finally, we caravanned to the mountains in two cars in order to contain not only our month's supplies but enough carriers to bring along our third cat, Jeremy. We traveled out of state as well—to Canada many times, Alaska, and Tahiti.

As he turned seventy-nine, we could see that caring for the huge yard through the Arizona summers was becoming too large a task, and we knew it was time, after forty years, to leave our beloved home. Two weeks before moving, we took the black cat Boston into our family, who for some time had been circling the house, meowing and nibbling on the food we left outside. With our now four cats, we moved to a townhome in the suburbs, with a patio and balcony overlooking a lake.

One day, not too long after, he asked me to go upstairs. When he would give me the signal, I was to come out to the balcony. I was in for another surprise. He was standing below in Elizabethan cape and feathered hat. And he delighted me with a recitation of the entire Romeo speech, "But soft, what light through yonder window breaks?" He was forever the true Romantic!

That fall, for our fiftieth wedding anniversary, we cruised the Hawaiian Islands, with side trips to zip-line and kayak, our last little adventures. We settled in to a quiet life on the lake with our four cats.

Looking back through the mist of time, I tend to characterize the life we lived as a fairy-tale existence, for I know now, better than ever before, that I had the privilege of sharing my life with a man who had the power to bring a special magic into the lives of others, to draw forth beauty and poetry from the ordinary and allow us to see with new eyes. But no tale of magic is without its shadow. There were many conflicts, and one by one we moved through them together. Divorce was never an option. We knew we couldn't bear to be apart. My constant fear, throughout my life, was losing him. His greatest concern was how I would live without him.

The shadow of dissolution began to lengthen across our lives. It was not long after we moved that I realized he was having problems remembering, and a slow terror began to creep over me.

We developed a friendship with a young couple on our street who shared his sense of playfulness. He reprised his bunny role for them at Easter and took a turn around the neighborhood in the costume as well. The day was hot. Later, he told me with sadness in his eyes as he shrugged out of the costume, "I can't do this anymore. It's too much." Fatigue began to take over his life, and as his memory receded, he grew more tired, sleeping many hours during the day. Yet he never lost his sense of humor. A neighbor told me years later that one day as he was taking his slow walk to the end of the street, she and a girlfriend, walking on either side of her husband, passed by him. He didn't know them well but said quietly, not even turning his head to greet them, "It is good to see that plural marriage is alive and well in Arizona." She said at first they were mildly stunned and then burst out laughing. Although his memory continued to fade through the years, I am so grateful that he never forgot me.

Lessons in Poetry

    We had lived eight years in the townhome by the lake when one day as he was watering the plants on the patio, he spotted a small branch on the bank of the lake that the gardeners had neglected to collect. As he tried to navigate the steep slope to pick it up, he took a bad fall. After six weeks in rehab, he had been home for only a few days when I took him for a brief stay in hospice, so that they could stabilize his sleep medications. He never came home. On October 13, 2012, after fifty-eight years of marriage, my world changed forever.

Chapter 2

The shadow that death casts is long and deep. There is a gloom that hovers, that envelops the soul, gives rise to unreasonable fears that torture the mind and rip at the already-battered heart. During long nights without him, I would lie in bed and repeat the lines from "The Raven," as I did when I was yet a girl, lying with my head in his lap. Within Poe's words were captured the terror, the grief, the despair that now filled my soul. The raven's beak had pierced my heart.

Now that he was gone, I had no desire to stay. I felt I was trapped in a bubble of illusion, and outside of it was the whole spirit world of which he was a part. I wanted to burst free as I sobbed on my knees to the powers that be, "Release me from this prison!" My mind held me captive, playing and replaying troubled memories of all the ways I had failed him during his last weeks on earth and all the times I had thoughtlessly hurt him during our lifetime. I spoke into the darkness of night, hoping somehow he was listening, begging his forgiveness and declaring my love for him in all the phases of his moods and all the stages of his life, a love that I felt more intensely than ever before. I was relentless in judging my wrongdoings over the span of a lifetime, feeling that a force beyond me had set in motion a remembrance of past error that I was powerless to stop. It caused me to wonder if I was working alongside him as he completed his own life review.

It was as if I clung to a wild pendulum that carried me from one pole to another: from affirming that I was committed to dying to wondering how I could create a life for myself; from asking, *How can I let go without forgetting?* to insisting that I could not move on without letting go; from a deep, sobbing sadness that screamed I could never be happy without him to a calm recognition that solitude was what I needed to come home to my soul.

I read the poems I had written over the years that asserted the union of two souls together through millennia. It seemed the poems carried a wisdom that I no longer possessed. What I needed most was a reaffirmation that we were together even in the moment of my deepest grief. At the same time that I was yearning for connection, begging for him to come to me, the skeptic within me continued to strike down every effort he made at contact. I held fast to the belief that I was not intuitive, that I was unable to see past the veil.

Just days after his passing, a friend in a distant city, Neva, called me to tell me that he had seemed to shake her by the shoulder when she was meditating, saying, "Tell her I did not die. I am with her." I longed to believe her, but I wanted my own experience of him. Yet, when it came, I argued against it. One night, when I was in a hypnogogic fog, he seemed to tug at me, trying to pull me from the bed. I discounted the incident as a dream, even though I had spoken aloud, asking him to let me sleep. I had felt certain I was awake. Yet I failed to ask a most revealing question, "Is that state, where one is poised in the doorway between sleep and waking, indeed, an open sesame to another realm?"

There were other moments just as strange, instants that were like a stroke of lightning that illuminates the darkness, revealing, with consummate clarity, a hitherto unseen figure lingering nearby. One night, drifting off to sleep, I was suddenly standing in the bathroom, when in an electric flash, he appeared before me, every detail of his form starkly defined and imprinted on my mind before the vision faded. Startled, I sat up, confused by being back in bed.

Another time, as I woke from a dream, I saw him standing at the foot of a stair, his face full of sadness as he said, "They crossed and left me behind." Even as the skeptic in me refused to acknowledge these incidents as real, this last impression troubled me greatly. I had crafted a mental narrative of what was happening to him in the spirit world. Now, a fear rose in me that my inability to move on was holding him back as well, that even though we were unable to touch, we lived in parallel worlds.

The night after this incident, I awoke at 3:25 a.m. from a puzzling dream. In the dream, I am running alone, barefoot over green hills—hill after hill. Suddenly, I start to lift above the ground—there is a duck flying low, and I soar high above it. I am flying by using powerful, pumping wing strokes. My head is like that of a strange bird or gargoyle. I shout, "I am Phoenix," and have a sense of great power and motion as I come awake. It would be months before I received a clue as to the significance of the dream, and even then, I doubted.

Calls from my friends came further and further apart. I was lonely, but I was unable to pick up the phone to issue an invitation, so I sat long days, paralyzed, ruminating, telling myself over and over what I should do, yet I was helpless to do it. I asked, "Where is that part of me that can reach out? Be myself?" But I wondered if I even knew who that self was. I questioned the loyalty of my friends, felt abandoned in my hour of need, yet I knew that a cloak of dark energy clung to me and that no one could bear for long the somberness of my grieving spirit. I wrote in my journal.

January 13, 2013

> Three months today that I have been without him, and in that time, I have seen the crumbling of my world, the complete emptiness of my life, the baseless self I am, without any anchor, a lost soul who can connect with nothing.
>
> I thought often of the lonely days during the fifteen months we had spent apart before we were married, how I had anticipated his distant homecoming. Where there was hope then, there was only despair now. Yet my tormented thoughts began to give mystical

significance to that time period, and I kept count of the weeks as they passed, toward what end I didn't know.

Although my spirit was ensnared in a shadow of self-doubt and I slogged through the days as through a viscous atmosphere that continued to drag me down, I made efforts to find solace for my near mortally wounded soul. I ordered books on dream work and after-death experience, signed up for a grief seminar, and searched for a private counselor. I hoped that reaching out in my dreams and working to develop my intuition might put me in touch with him. That intention, to reunite with him in spirit, became the focus of my life. Even though my efforts were rewarded from the beginning, my disbelief and inability to trust my own wisdom kept me from accepting my own experience.

The very day after I had resolved to put all my effort toward making connection with him, I began a familiar interior monologue as I was driving. "I have nothing to live for; there is nothing to look forward to; I have no goals, no joy, no life."

His voice brought me up short: "But wait!"

At first, I was startled, but then I began to laugh. It was one of those silly games we had shared, applying that phrase to a variety of situations, mocking the infomercials that used the line repeatedly. How appropriate to remind me in this way that my life did have purpose and that already here was the connection I was seeking.

Yet I took neither of these messages to heart. I continued to look for evidence that he was with me and never ceased to mourn that he was not. Neither my body nor my brain were functioning well. I lost weight and energy, slept for long hours during the night, and sat listless for long hours during the day. I forgot appointments or showed up an hour early or half hour late. I could not remember what I planned to do in the next moment and began to entertain fears that I was losing my memory. My dreams were filled with episodes of forgetfulness, forgetting whom I was supposed to meet, where I had left my car, how to get back to the place I had just left. As in those dreams, I had no sense of continuity in my life. I felt as if I were sleepwalking, playing some part in a play, acting out a role that is expected, that of a normal, happy person. But I came home to the reality—where I was desolated, disconsolate, wondering how I could get up from the chair and go on stage again. I identified with the Greek mourner, Niobe, frozen in stone forever as tears of grief continued to trickle from her eyes.

Decades before, I had made some successful experiments in lucid dreaming, and so I began to focus on my dreams. Not long after in another dream, I awaken to find him beside me. In the dream, I celebrate the moment and say to myself, "It is him. He is here." Another time, I awoke with an intense sense of his presence in the room, and on opening my eyes to find myself alone, I broke into sobs. Again and again, I dreamed of poignant moments in which I felt his presence, yet the sweetness of the dream only intensified the horror when I would awake to the stark reality that he was no longer in the world. Then one night I had a very real dream of him acting out a scene from *Laurel and Hardy*, a favorite of his, and I woke up laughing. He had always loved to make me laugh. And I thought for the first time, *Truly, he is with me in my dreams*. As I dozed again, I had the distinct impression that I was resting my head peacefully on his shoulder.

I arose the next morning to prepare for my first visit with Janet, a psychologist of profound insight and compassion who was to guide me through the next years with a gentle and loving hand. She was the first who seemed to understand what I was going through. She validated the sense I had that he was with me the night before and shared her own similar experiences. I left her feeling a glimmer of hope that I might one day connect with him.

April arrived—and indeed, it was the cruelest month—heralding his birthday, the palo verde bursting forth to blossom golden color all along the avenues as it cast sunlit shadows over the bougainvillea and lantana already in full bloom. Nature's celebration of spring underlined the irony that he was no longer here to share its beauty with me, only deepening my despair and the immense sadness of a life without him. And all the things in the world that were special to him were triggers of sadness for me.

The blue heron was one exception. When we lived on the desert mountain, we would travel to the Verde River in the spring to witness the spectacle of blue herons nesting. The cottonwoods were decorated with a hundred huge nests where the giant birds would alight, bringing fish to their young. He never tired of visiting the river where the herons brought a special joy to his heart. And when we moved to the lake, he was delighted that, on occasion, we were visited by a lone blue heron. It would come by our back patio, strutting along the edge of the lake, the webs in its large feet spreading as it planted them in the grass, the head thrusting forward on the long neck with every stride of its stilt-like legs. On the ground, it seemed a bit of a clown, but when it took to the sky, I marveled at its grace and beauty, the broad wings seeming to span the lake as it skimmed the water. I came to love the heron as his symbol and his true messenger. There were times in the months that followed that I would be grumbling to myself that I should give up hope of ever getting in touch with him when the heron would appear—on my morning walk, I might see it high in the sky, or in the evening as I looked out over the patio to the lake, it would sail into my line of vision. I believed that he sent it to give me hope. It always brought a measure of comfort.

But such moments were brief. I was haunted by the fear that he would not wait for me, or that so much time would pass, while I lingered here, that the movement of his world would take him completely out of my realm. And sleep was no respite, for there my fears would follow me by surfacing in dreams of his leaving, or disappearing, or dying one more time. One night, he was suddenly beside me. I could feel his presence. Although he seemed younger, I felt more than saw him. I spoke to him, asking, "Please come back to me."

He answered, "No."

And I forced the issue. "Don't you love me anymore?"

"That's not it," he told me. "You are better off without me."

I protested, "How can you say that when I am grieving every minute of the day?" Yet I had the feeling that he knew more about it than I did. On coming fully awake, I couldn't shake the sense that I hadn't been asleep. I felt as if he had actually been with me.

Yet dreams about him grew further and further apart. And with this gradual ceasing of nightly dreams about him, new fears arose that he was slipping away from me—that I would have to face my life without him, that our time together was over and could not be retrieved, no matter how hard I tried to hang onto it in my dreams. Yet I could not force myself to want to be here. Eight months had passed, and I continued to feel brokenhearted, split off from my source. At times, I would stop crying for several days as an empty numbness coursed through me. I felt like a hollow shell, walking, talking, pretending to be a person who lives and breathes. And then the wrenching upset would surge again. I would tell myself that my loss was irretrievable, that the joy of being with him would never return, that there would always be anguish within me that could arise at any moment. Every day would be a struggle, and I would have no choice but to endure. I was still physically depleted. To live life was a battle, and I was exhausted from it. Accepting the numerous manifestations of connection that occurred became easier, but they were so fleeting that they cheered me only for a moment.

Most of all, I wanted some confirmation that he would wait for me. The notion that I would be left behind plagued me. I feared that as he moved deeper and deeper into that vast world of spirit, it would be he who would forget me. I trembled at the thought that when I arrived on that misty shore, my love would not be there to greet me. One morning as I went into meditation with the question on my mind, "Will you wait for me?" I fell into a hypnogogic state. Suddenly, in one of those lightning flashes, I found myself driving into the garage, and in that instant, he was standing before the car, waiting for me to come home. In that demonstration of how often he had waited for me in life was an assurance that, as always, he would wait for me still.

I continued, twice weekly, to share those fears with Janet. Yet, one day, in a more cheerful mood, I told her about many of the surprises he had arranged for me during our lifetime. I related how he had crafted poems to me and written welcome signs in flowers for my homecomings. In response, she had admonished me to remember those beautiful gifts. Knowing that I loved to write, she suggested I write a memoir honoring his life.

In that moment, she planted a seed that refused to die. As time passed, I considered her suggestion with growing excitement. I began to contemplate writing a memorial to our love. Even though I was unaware of it, my life was shifting toward hope.

One of the events I had told her about was that golden autumn day long ago when he had staged the verse from *The Rubaiyat of Omar Khayyam* by laying out the picnic of bread, wine, and the book of verse. For days after, I kept remembering the little book of verse that he had used as a part of that scene. He had read to me from it many times in the early days of our relationship, but there was one poem that kept tugging at my mind. I could remember only a fragment of the verse and little of what it was about, but I felt a great urgency to find it. I searched through our library until I came across that precious, worn paperback, pages hanging loosely from its spine, and I thumbed through them, hoping to retrieve the lost poem. But I quickly realized the difficulty of the task. I had only two clues, something about flinging a pellet of clay and what I thought was a direct quotation, "It could have happened once, once only." Googling those lines brought me nothing.

Over the next few days, I continued to return to Google with a different version of the lines. At last, desperate, I committed to read through every suggestion a site listed, and finally, there it was, buried on the back pages in a mountain of entries, "Youth and Art," by Robert Browning. And there was the line that, again and again, I had tried to recall:

> Why did you not pinch a flower
> In a pellet of clay and fling it?

With a bit of humor, it tells the story of a pair of young artists, she a singer, he a sculptor, who lived on the same street and would watch each other from a distance going about their lives. They felt an attraction yet never came together. He went on to be knighted for his talents, and she married into wealth, but their lives were nevertheless unfulfilled. The singer, who is the narrator, mourns:

> We have not sighed deep, laughed free
> Starved, feasted, despaired—been happy.
>
> And nobody calls you dunce,
> And people suppose me clever;
> This could have happened once,
> And we missed it, lost it forever.

She still felt the attraction, saw him even as a soul mate, perhaps, and realized the magnitude of what was lost. As I finished this verse that he had shared with me so long ago, I felt the immensity of my own loss and in the next instant an elation in knowing that we had missed nothing. And in a moment of what seemed like great insight, I felt he had offered me, years ago, a mysterious caveat, which said, "Look at what could happen to us. Don't let this opportunity pass." As tears streamed down my face, I felt the familiar wrenching grief and, at once, an ecstasy in recognizing, for the first time since my loss, what a great gift my life had brought me—years of joy and companionship with a beloved soul mate. And I sobbed, "We seized the moment. We did not let it slip away!"

Chapter 3

The recognition of the gift I had been given, although welcome, did not dispel my despair. My birthday had come and gone, the first without him. As time moved toward the milestone of the anniversary of his passing, and difficult memories arose to torture my mind, I moved deeper into grief. Convention advised me to let go and get on with my life. I didn't feel it. I didn't want it. My heart continued to whisper, "He is my soul mate." I yearned only for connection, feeling that the grief, the tears, the place where memories seared my soul with longing and desire were what joined me to him. And I looked to Rumi.

> The grief you cry out from
> draws you toward union …
>
> Listen to the moan of a dog for its master.
> That whining is the connection.
>
> There are love dogs
> no one knows the names of.
>
> Give your life
> to be one of them.[4]

---

[4] Translation by Coleman Barks, *The Essential Rumi: New Expanded Edition* (New York: HarperCollins, 2004), 155–156.

I asked again and again, "Why am I still here?" I wondered if our two cats, Jeremy and Boston, were the reason. When we had rescued them from the street, it was our silent commitment to be there throughout their lifetimes. It was I who was left to fulfill that pledge. "Or," I would question, "am I here to write our story? Is that even important? Or am I being made to stay until I can say goodbye to him? Do I ever have to say goodbye?" Janet reminded me of the many partings and reunions we had had over a lifetime and suggested that even though this separation seemed permanent, in the context of eternity, it was just one more parting. Did I doubt that there would be yet another reunion?

As I clung to the hope of being again with him, I moved to sharpen my intuitive skills, signing up for a series of one-on-one sessions with a psychic whom I had encountered years before. During a meditation, she took me through a process in which I was to meet and ask the name of my guide. I was disappointed to have to tell her that his name was Homer, as an image of Homer Simpson sprang to mind, hardly a transcendent figure. As she prodded me for other Homers I might have known, I thought of Homer, the ancient Greek poet, a much more appropriate figure for a guide. I took home the assignment to visit him during my meditations and ask questions of him. During the first session, he seemed to be wearing a black cloak with a hood that almost hid his face. I asked him several questions; most of his replies were transparently my own hastily invented answers. At last, I gave in to my curiosity and asked, "Why do you look like a death figure?" The answer came like lightning, "To lead you out of this place of death." I felt as if his reply had come from a different place, and I began to believe that this phantom might carry some truths for me. It was clear that I had been long in the place of death, from weeping through nights in its shadow to feeling nothing but emptiness inside. I returned a few more times to query him. When I asked, prompted by the psychic, "What do I need to know that I already know?" I didn't receive an immediate response. But that night, I dreamed I was flying. As I awoke, I was associating my flying self with intuition, and the answer came, "I am intuitive." At last I was ready to receive this answer.

Sadly, I didn't pursue this relationship with the sage of my meditations. But the penultimate time I consulted him, he offered me information that has continually supported me in learning to trust myself. Through the summer, a prickling sensation in my scalp during meditation became more and more pronounced. Finally, I put the question to Homer, "What does it mean when my scalp tingles?" The answer was brief but profound, "It is the perception of a truth." As it came, my scalp thrilled from my forehead all the way to the nape of my neck, and I knew it was a true answer, one even I could not doubt.

I continued my sessions with the psychic even though I was in the midst of a series of cluster migraines, which brought about, even between headaches, a constant state of disorientation, fogginess of thinking, and a deepening depression. That dark energy began to gather more heavily around me and exacerbated my fears that I would never see him again. It was on October 12, the day before the anniversary of his passing, that I attended a lecture. Richard Martini, a filmmaker, spoke about the experiences chronicled in his book, *Flipside: A Tourist's Guide on How to Navigate the Afterlife*. I was familiar with literature on reincarnation, but this information was new to me. The life between lives was a whole realm that I knew nothing about. I learned that there was a cadre of professionals trained by the Newton Institute who were routinely regressing clients into a place where they could recall a time, between lives on earth, that they had spent in the spirit world.

Suddenly, new hope sprang within me. Was there a possibility that I could consult such a person and thus find a way to see Johnny? Perhaps even a short visit with him would dispel my fears and assure me that I would be with him again, making it bearable for me to live in the world. I grew more excited as the lecture progressed and squirmed in my seat until the Q&A when I could ask him for the name of someone with the expertise to take me there.

As I stood in line waiting for Martini to autograph my book, I contemplated the reference he had made during the lecture to the myth of the phoenix bird that had been reborn from its own ashes, and I remembered my own dream where I had flown as a huge bird, crying, "I am Phoenix." I spoke to Martini for a few moments as he signed my book and impulsively told him of my dream. He shot back at me with unhesitating assurance that the bird in flight was my husband. Taken aback by this comment, I walked away in disbelief, puzzling at why he would say such a thing. Yet when I peeked into what I had written in my journal nine months earlier about the dream of the phoenix, I discovered that just the night before, I had the vision of Johnny telling me he had been left behind. Was the phoenix dream a message to calm my fears aroused by that vision? If so, I had failed completely to connect the two. Perhaps the ecstasy I had felt in flight was the joy in knowing that he was free.

Almost at once, I moved to get in touch with a woman in Sedona who had been trained in the Newton method. I hoped she might help me make contact with Johnny through regressing me into a life between lives. If I had no success in reaching him through dreams, perhaps here was another way.

Even as I had these thoughts, I was dreaming frequently of him. One night, I dreamed he had been away at war and had been through a great trauma. We had been separated for a long while and retired to a peaceful place with lovely gardens where Penelope, a cat we once owned, was free to wander. It was a place where we both could rehabilitate from a long, difficult time. Did this dream represent a healing for us both? I awoke feeling hopeful. A few nights later, I lay half in slumber as I seem to be following him through an unfamiliar house. I cannot see him, but I hear him speak, asking me if I have enough money to live on. I tell him yes, I have plenty. He asks about a specific bill, and I tell him I can pay it. He moves through a hallway, and I wonder if I should follow him there. I fear if I do, I will find him gone, because it is hard for me to believe that he has come back. As I came fully awake, my heart was pounding. I felt he had been with me.

In the meantime, I had reached an agreement with the therapist in Sedona. It was necessary that I schedule two all-day sessions a week apart, the first a past-life regression that would prepare me for the second and desired one. I made a reservation at a hotel in Sedona for the night before my appointment so that I could arrive early enough for an all-day session and then drive back to Phoenix in the evening. In the meantime, I was to prepare by completing a thought-provoking questionnaire and listening to recordings she had provided.

A week before I was to travel to Sedona, I had dinner with a friend and excitedly told her of my plans. During our conversation, she asked what I would do if I learned in the regression that Johnny and I had finished our relationship. She had reached deep and touched the fear of my most terrible imaginings. I tried to rationalize her dark suggestion away, seeking to convince myself that it could never be so. The next day, I dropped my hand mirror, which seemed to leap from my grasp. *What does that mean?* I asked. *Shattered hopes? Shattered life? No mirror for myself?* He was my mirror.

The Monday that I was to drive to Sedona approached, and all weekend, a foreboding burgeoned within me. Sunday evening at 7:30, I got a migraine headache. I knew how difficult it would be to rise early and drive that distance with the lingering effects of the headache. I knew I was not supposed to go, yet it was so hard to give up what I saw as my one last hope. I wrote in my journal:

November 23, 2013

    I think my soul is not ready for this. I guess I am going to have to succumb to being unable to reach him and plod away until my life is over. I am so disappointed. I feel I have let myself down. I have had this terrible foreboding that I am taking on more than I can handle, and I need to learn not to repeat an error that I have made many times in my life. I want to be more than I am.

The next morning, early, with my head still pounding, I called the therapist in Sedona to cancel, knowing that I was letting her down as badly as I was myself. I was robbing her of an entire day that she could have made other appointments.

Added to my deep grief, the stress of that decision brought on a string of headaches that kept me in a migraine fog from Thanksgiving into the following February. It was a time of intense depression and continued soul-searching. The urge to write was there, but I could not believe I would ever write again. Even more pressing was the worry that I was holding him too closely. I told myself I must stop focusing on my loneliness and give my attention to my love for him without conditions. The end of 2013 came and went. It was for me only a marker of a year passing, which did not have him as part of its history, and a new year arriving that was not worth celebrating without him in it.

A couple of months before, I had driven for a ways alongside a little red sports car, which conjured memories of an Austen-Healey Sprite I had seen in a showroom window in 1959. We were living in Pendleton, Oregon, where Johnny was teaching, but he was away for nearly the whole summer at a Spanish institute in Virginia. Because we had so often dreamed of owning an Austen-Healey sports car, which was way beyond our means, I couldn't wait to tell him about this darling little car with "bug eye" headlights perched on its "bonnet" and a very affordable price tag. I shot off a letter extolling its benefits, especially in light of our plans for him to begin graduate school the next year. The advantage in gas mileage alone over our Plymouth would mean significant savings, to say nothing of the joy of owning a little red sports car. When he at last got to see the car, it didn't take him a minute to accept my proposal, and it was not long before we found ourselves, with the top unsnapped and stored behind the bucket seats, skimming low along the highway. We kept the car through four years of graduate school at the University of Oregon, and after we moved to Phoenix, he drove it to ASU, where he taught, for sixteen years. It was our intention to save this classic car for our son, Sean, but sadly, it was stolen from the ASU parking lot on his tenth birthday. Looking over at the little red Mazda in the traffic lane next to me, I idly dreamed of having such a car and putting on its license plate, in memory of his performance poetry, "La Luna." An idea was born in that moment, and I decided, even if I couldn't have a red sports car, at least I could have a license plate that honored him.

A month after, I sat down at the computer. The DMV website gave immediate feedback. "La Luna" was taken. I offered a variety of ideas linked to his interest in Spanish poetry. None were available. I had given some thought to conjuring a bit of magic by declaring a present connection with him. "In touch," "N touch," and "N tuch" all were nixed by the program in the computer. *And justifiably so,* I thought, *since it is not true that I am in touch with him.* I stared blankly at the screen, having exhausted a list of suggestions I had compiled over the last month. Then, one of those sudden ideas urged my fingers to type BWITHME. And just as quickly, the word *available* sprang onto the screen. The speed of that action left me nonplussed for a moment, until the fear arose that asking him to stay was just another way of hanging on. I turned off the computer without reserving the letters. And yet my heart had spoken. I wanted that license plate so much. I vacillated for days and finally stole back to the DMV website, hoping those words had not been snatched away. When I found they had not, I ordered at once, before I could change my mind.

Over the long months, I had continued the countdown to January 13, 2014, the date that would mark the second fifteen-month-long period in my life that I had spent without him. I waited with a certain expectation to see what would happen. On January 12, the new license plate arrived. If somewhere in the recesses of my mind I understood the significance of that convergence, I did not acknowledge it. I unwrapped the license plate and let it lay on the kitchen island for several days, afraid to take the final step. Finally, as I knelt behind my car to loosen the screws on the old plate, I was filled with trepidation, realizing that there was no turning back. I was at last declaring my intention. I was through trying to let him go. I was asking him to stay—to be with me.

I wish I could say that this step lifted my spirits and gave me new purpose. But for the next three months, I was awash in regret and despair. It seemed impossible for me to do anything. I felt as if I were pushing through a syrupy atmosphere, slogging through muddy terrain. For days on end, I would seem to dive into a well of grief and, at last, come up for air and float on the surface, feeling dead inside. Instead of meditating, I ranted against spirit, feeling I was a victim of a soul who had sacrificed me to suffer so she could learn. I even, on occasion, forgot my address, my phone number. My life was in pieces, no more understandable than a jigsaw puzzle just dumped out of the box.

And the license plate, now on my car for all to see, was still an issue for me. A friend looked at it and asked, "For Johnny?" When I nodded, she spoke my name in that parental tone used with children to say, you know better. And there were many who said nothing, but their very silence spoke of their belief that I should let him go. It was hard not to believe that they were right.

For several months, I had thought about seeing a medium, but as with the therapist in Sedona, I was afraid of what I would learn. What if that person were to tell me he no longer loved me or had moved on to another life? Maybe I would discover he was not really my soul mate, even though I had long had the sense that I had been with him since the beginning of time.

Yet in all the fear and sadness, there were momentary bright spots. One night as I was reading in bed, I started to doze and heard him laughing, as close as if he rested on the pillow beside me. It brought me awake so quickly that I didn't hear what he had started to say. And I dreamed of the joy of seeing him healthy and strong or feeling him come up behind me and hold me close. One day, as I walked up the path to the front door, a bougainvillea blossom rolled along ahead of me, and I knew that he had sent it. It rests today in a dish among my mementos, perfectly preserved.

As the wheel of the year turned and April came again, I thought that if I wished him to communicate with me, perhaps I should make an effort to speak to him. Remembering how I had written him every day for the fifteen months that he had spent in Spain the first time, I decided to take a while each evening, as I had in that distant past, to share my thoughts with him. At first, I burned the letters at sunset in a symbolic gesture to send my words to spirit. But soon, as more and more I poured out my heart to him, I kept them.

The day before his birthday, I wrote in my journal:

April 26, 2014

> The day is clouded over. It is in the low seventies, a chilly day for late April, with a gentle wind blowing. So like many days and evenings we spent together, when I first knew him. And I hear the leaves, which fall from our tree much of the year, rustling on the patio, reminding me of chilly autumn nights long ago, when leaves tumbled along the dimly lighted streets of Portland before the wind. Such feeling rises in me as I recall those precious times in which a sadness at every brief parting dwelled even then—a prefiguring of all the days I have spent without him. There is such nostalgia for the days we were together in the dreary weather. And such an aching for him, wanting to be with him, wanting him here with me now—like then. And I tell myself, "You should not sit here next to the open door. You should slam it shut, go upstairs, and insulate yourself from this cloudy day, so heavy with memories. Go to the computer where you can't hear the wind, nor feel the familiar dampness of the day that stirs those longings so strongly. But I can't tear myself away from the deep beauty that resides there within my Romantic spirit, a part of me I refuse to deny, that I cherish because it is what I share most deeply with him.

On the morning of his birthday, I awoke to that same sadness. As I got ready to walk, I pushed down the tears that sought to rise in my throat. When I opened the door to step outside, I broke into a fit of sobbing, and the walk was aborted as I fell into a chair and began to cry out to him for a sign that he was with me. And then I said out loud to myself, "Don't be stupid. No one as despairing as I is ever given epiphanies or manifestations, and certainly not miracles. It's foolish to ask." At that moment, I caught a glimpse of a giant blue wing outside the window. Could it be the blue heron was landing? I hadn't seen it for nine months. I hurried outside, fearing the one glimpse would be all I would have. But no. I watched it stride deliberately down the bank until it flew again, stretching its broad wings across the sky. My spirits were lifted on those wings. Such a magical bird! Such a magical moment! What a wonderful gift Johnny had given me on his birthday! In that second, I did not doubt. With new hope, I wrote him that night. "May you know joy in every moment, may you know happiness without end, and, if it please the universe, may I spend eternity with you. Thank you for being with me."

Chapter 4

If in one moment I believed that he was answering my call for help and sending me a sign, in the next I was doubting the very message I had prayed for. I feared I had been carried away with my own fanciful thinking. Yet my very existence seemed to depend on finding a way to communicate with him, and because I would not trust myself to hear him, I felt compelled to find someone who could. Although I had visited channels and psychics in the past, I had shied away from those who claimed to speak with the dead. Now, my most viable option seemed to be to visit a medium. Although I had been thinking about it for some time, my fears of what I might learn had held me back. I wanted to believe that we were soul mates and had been together since the beginning of time but feared it was just my own fantasy. What I wanted to hear was confirmation of that hope, that he still loved me and wanted to be with me. What if I were to be told that none of this was true and that he didn't wish to see me again? I had read of people who had received such brutal news through mediums.

The opportunity seemed thrust upon me when I was at the very point of seeking it out. As I stopped into a neighborhood bookstore one day, a flier posted at the counter caught my attention: "Reunions with those we've loved and lost." The bookstore owner told me that the reunions were group sessions directed by a medium who gave spontaneous readings to participants. It was the very thing I had been considering, yet fear still hovered in the shadows. To bolster my courage, I persuaded a skeptical friend, Priscilla, to go there with me the following Friday to hear the medium, Jamie Clark.

Arriving early, we made our way to the back of the bookstore, where about twenty-five chairs were stuffed into a small room. We took seats in the first row, and for the next half hour, my stomach tight with anticipation, I watched people arrive and the room gradually fill to capacity. At last, at 7:00 sharp, Jamie walked into the room. Of average height, with soft eyes and short, spiked hair sporting an orange tint, he was dressed simply in jeans and a blue T-shirt. After bowing his head briefly, he spoke rapidly to us, giving an outline of how he worked and telling us that he would focus wherever his attention was drawn. His gaze moved about the room, and he began to speak to particular people, asking first whether there was a sister, a father, or a grandmother who had passed.

His readings were sometimes lighthearted, often entertaining, but did not lack compassion. As he spoke to one person, then another, I watched the minutes crawl by, fearing that I would be chosen and, at the same time, that I would not. An hour had passed when Jamie looked directly at me and asked, "Is your husband passed?" Mute, I nodded. "He has been waiting for a long time to speak," Jamie told me. "Whether you were married for a short time or a long while is not the thing. You have been together for a very, very long time. You are soul mates."

These few words were balm to my soul. Tears sprang to my eyes as a great relief flooded through me. There was nothing Jamie could have said that would have touched me more deeply, nor convinced me more fully that Johnny was speaking to me, calming my fears and my grief. The moment validated not only that he knew what was happening in my life but also that the bond of our love was still intact and that my intuition had been accurate.

Jamie went on to make references to Johnny's teaching and writing, his distinctive voice and striking eyes, his recent birthday, the significance of the month of October. He even mentioned a piano, which in years past had been the subject of a standing joke between Johnny, Priscilla, and me. I thought pointing to a situation that had involved our friend who was present was his way of communicating that he was quite aware of what was going on in the room. Jamie then urged us all to communicate with our loved ones, because, he said, they were eager to hear from us.

In that moment, the tenor of my life shifted. I at last believed his spirit was with me, and I opened my heart to receive his messages—those signs I had been denying for eighteen long months. At times, in deep meditation, I would sense that he was speaking to me, and at other times, I seemed to feel his presence, accompanied by that tingling on the crown of my head. I concluded that I had sensed his presence many times but failed to recognize it.

The next month, I attended Jamie's group session again, and it did not disappoint. Jamie intuited that I wrote to Johnny and told me that he had received the letters and (Jamie kissed his fingers) they were sealed with a kiss. He spoke for a second time of how well Johnny communicates with people and told me he is a Romantic. I smiled and nodded.

Soon after, I sat on the patio, for the first time since he had gone, to have my coffee. It was an early morning in June, and the air was still crisp. The sun sparkled on the water. As I began to muse on what he might be doing, I had a sudden vision of him dancing with Lorca, the Spanish poet he had spent his life studying. It was a transcendent moment of pure joy for me, to think of him there living his dream. After I meditated that morning, I jotted down the first lines I had written in years:

Dancing with Lorca

And are you now
Dancing with Lorca?
Clothed only in moonlight,
Flowing through eons of poetry
To a gypsy beat.

> Or are you now
> Poised in a timeless room,
> Suspended in a seminal breath
> Of inspiration and communion
> With masters of a Spanish art?
>
> Or do you review?
> Riffling pages of the rapid years
> That chronicled flamenco rhythms,
> And only whispered shadows
> Of twin souls entwined.
>
> Or do you create
> In secret? As master of surprise,
> Disguise discarded to reveal,
> In full Alhambran splendor,
> Your own magnificence in bloom.

That evening, as I wrote my letter, I asked him, "Did you like my poem?" and his voice at once spoke within my mind, saying, "Dun't ask" in Tony Soprano style. I laughed out loud. It was so real and so exactly the humorous answer he had often given me in life.

In writing the poem, I perceived for the first time that poetry originated from a different place than ordinary thought. It was an exhilarating experience, and my spirits soared for a few days. But I was to learn that the deep well of sadness within me would draw me back into depression again and again. Grief was not through with me yet. I had not changed my mind about wanting to die in order to be with him. I was quick to say so. And I had told Janet numerous times that the only way I could be happy on earth was to be in clear and constant communication with him. Nothing else would satisfy.

Because Jamie's reunions had, for the first time, put language to the vague impressions I received and brought me at least temporary comfort, I began to see him from time to time for the rest of that year. He asked me, on a couple of occasions, if I had a shirt of Johnny's. I affirmed that I did, and yes, it had the vertical and horizontal stripes that Jamie had described, as it was a plaid shirt. When I had washed his clothes for the last time, I had hung the shirt in my closet, because it was his favorite. I wanted to keep it near me, even wear it. But when I had put it on, months after his passing, I broke into agonized sobs and sank to the floor, overcome with longing for his physical presence. Jamie said that Johnny wanted me to put it on because it was a way for him, effortlessly, to wrap his loving energy around me. When at last I wore the shirt again, there was sadness in it, but I felt his deep love and comfort as well.

In June, I scheduled a private reading with Jamie that brought me hope as well as puzzlement. He spoke at length about my communication with Johnny and told me gently that I needed to release the old connection of feeling alone and that nobody was listening. Only then could I move to a new connection of "complete soul communication and integration." He told me that I didn't need to try so hard, that Johnny had been channeling energy to me for the last six months. I noted that it had been just six months before that I had posted BWITHME on my license plate. I thought, perhaps, in that act, I had opened a conduit between us. I was perplexed when Jamie told me I was going to move from receiving communication through the senses to "multidimensional, physical-metaphysical vibrations." I had no idea what he meant. It would be a while before I would begin to understand.

Jamie had held out to me the possibility of forming a new kind of relationship, one of spirit rather than matter. To do this, he advised, I must turn my mind away from the reality of the ragged hole that gaped in the midst of my soul and think only on how, even now, he was with me and watched over me daily. Neither my will nor my imagination was powerful enough to do that. My nightly letters were filled with conflict between desiring this new way of being, above all, and the impossibility of accomplishing what was necessary to achieve it—letting go of the longing for his physical presence.

Yet I continued to explore the idea of a real spiritual relationship with him. Because the fear of holding him back was still of concern to me, one night I wrote to him:

July 10, 2014

> If what I have read is true, that only a portion of our spiritual energy comes here to earth, while the rest is engaged on the other side, surely, in the ever-present now, there is room for all things: for pursuit of your own learning, your own interests, your own life there with all of your friends and the poets you admired, a space to learn the things that you need to learn for your own growth, things that are not yet a part of my learning. And yet, is there not still time to drop in on me in the evening, during the day, and in my dreams? I am, hopefully, not keeping you from progressing. You know I wouldn't want that at all. But I wish some communication from you about this—I would like to achieve that place in our relationship where we can be in mutual agreement about what is needed.

The next day, as I checked my emails, I watched a cute-puppy video on YouTube that a friend had sent. When the video was over, the screen blinked and switched to a series of presentations by a psychic channel whose husband and partner had died. Randomly, I opened one of them in which she was speaking to an auditorium full of people, whom she and her husband had guided over the years. She was talking about her communication with him since he had gone, how she felt him beside her every moment of the day as she worked and in everything she did. She explained to the audience that he also could be with the hundreds of others who had followed him in life, and she spoke at length about how the energy of spirit is not confined to one place, one time.

I sat for a few minutes as what had just happened began to sink in. I had asked a question of Johnny yesterday, and just now, a perfectly direct answer had dropped from the sky into my computer. The grandness of this synchronous moment, at last, took hold. I had been given evidence I could not attribute to my imagination. There was, indeed, something new happening in our relationship, a definite uptick in the quality of our communication. I had received an answer that was so specific, so on target that I could not deny the truth of its message. What Jamie had promised seemed, at last, within the realm of the possible, although I had no idea of how it was to come to pass.

The excitement of receiving an answer carried me for a day or two, but it was not long before I was again in Janet's office complaining because I had not heard from him. She told me that it would serve me if I could learn to carry those moments of meeting in my heart rather than constantly looking for more. As much as I wanted to be satisfied and happy with what I was given, an occasional connection coming after long days of waiting did not fulfill my dream. I tried to surrender to how things were, often quoting to myself a line from Milton speaking of his blindness, "They also serve who only stand and wait." I felt it was my own blindness that kept me from seeing that Johnny's love was, in every moment, with me.

When he spoke to me again, it was in a rush of feeling carried by a powerful memory of his singing "Don't Cry for Me, Argentina," as he had often done. The loneliness that the recollection brought gave rise to sudden tears, yet almost immediately, I felt an inner prompting to review the words to the song. When I consulted Google and read them over, I saw the message in them—the promise that he would never leave me and the plea not to stay so far away. Was it I who was distancing myself from him?

It had been nearly a year now since Janet had suggested that I write a memoir honoring Johnny's life; the thought had continued to whisper to me, growing and changing as the days and months passed. I had begun to see more clearly the magnificence of his spiritual being, had learned to love him in a new way, so that Jamie's idea of a new relationship seemed plausible to me. In writing the poem "Dancing with Lorca," I felt I had glimpsed the world that he now lived in. Was it possible that I could experience it, experience him, even more fully? I asked him, "Do you think I am ready to write again? I know the work I want to do is a story of the magic of you and me." Even as I shared these dreams in my letters to him of how I wanted to write of a love that could conquer death and transcend time and space, I knew that our intentions must be aligned for this to happen. I could not set out on such a journey without knowing that he and I were walking a path together, hand in hand, perhaps not even knowing exactly where the path would lead. I feared he might think these were but overly romantic fantasies.

I had been preoccupied with such musings for several days when I went to a file cabinet to look for folders. I found none. I went through the drawers a second time, just to be sure, and a shoebox caught my eye. I peeked inside to find it was a box of greeting cards, apparently from family, as the top envelope had "Mom" printed on it. As I replaced the lid, I noticed, standing up and leaning against the box, another card. The envelope, in Johnny's printing, said "My True Love." My breath caught in my throat, for that phrase echoed the very words I had used to address him in my letter the night before. I opened the flap and slid the card out with trembling hands. A birthday card that he had given me the last years we were together seemed to have a carefully selected message:

> Once in a while, right in the middle of an ordinary life,
> Love gives us a fairy tale.
> I believe in magic,
> In happy-ever-afters
> And fantasies that really do come true—
> For seeing is believing,
> And I have living proof,
> Because I found forever love in you.

I was astounded. The card had such relevance to the moment. Again, an answer to what I had asked of him—a relationship that would continue the magic we had, one that would span matter and spirit and reach through the veil between our separate worlds to last through eternity. It affirmed his own belief in magic, in a love that lasts forever and fantasies that are real. To be at last assured that he was in full agreement with me about the nature of our relationship filled my heart, again, with joy.

Even though I felt confident that Johnny was in agreement with me, I was not ready to begin to write our story until my part in it had been fulfilled. I knew that I had nothing to say on this subject as long as I was mired in self-doubt much of the time. My own metamorphosis was needed into a person who could embrace life and be willing to live it fully. There could be no beginning until the ending was in sight. And so far, I could see no hope of such an ending. I could only move forward to find where my path would lead.

Within the two months since I had seen Jamie privately, one marvelous thing after another had happened. Most importantly, my relationship with Johnny had evolved so that we were now, I believed, in full agreement about how we wanted things to be between us. Most of my doubts about engaging him in this soul journey had been erased, and my biggest concern now was how to open my heart to hear him more clearly. Jamie had been so helpful in allowing me to believe this was possible that I sought him out once more.

He talked to me about the concept of neural soul ways, which, not unlike the neural pathways in the nervous system, were pathways for the feelings and language of the soul. He told me that Johnny was "impulsing" me to create these pathways and that the impulses would become stronger and stronger. These ideas made little sense to me at the time, but one thing Jamie said was startlingly clear to me. As I rose to leave, it seemed almost an afterthought when he said, "Oh, your husband is talking about you writing the book. He's like, 'Come on. Get moving.'" I had not told Jamie of my wish to write, for up to now I had wondered if I were nurturing an impossible dream. Yet it seemed that Johnny was urging me, through Jamie, to do just that. Nevertheless, I protested that I couldn't write until I had the ending. Jamie assured me that the ending would come to me and that Johnny would help me. I left thinking that the book would eventually come into being, but, considering the state of my consciousness, I believed that day was a long way off.

But other things that Jamie had spoken about began to manifest quickly. I had been communicating with Johnny each night by writing a letter. Now, I thought it wise to set aside a time to listen for what he had to say to me. Jamie had said that he could sense a beam of white light streaming from Johnny's heart to mine. One evening, nine days after I had visited him, I employed that image in my listening time. I began to visualize a beam of light that was symbolic to me of merging my heart with Johnny's heart, my soul with his. As I did this, the first lines from one of my poems came to me, "In that first forming cosmic fire/ I danced with you/ flame within flame." I began to recite the poem as I visualized our light, our hearts, our souls connecting. Suddenly, I felt a current, beginning at my left elbow, traveling at warp speed up my arm and across my shoulders to my right elbow. My shoulders shook with the force of the jolt. My eyes flew open. It was as if I had been struck by lightning! *Wow! That was fantastic,* I thought. At that moment, another shock wave, just as strong, traveled the same route.

I grabbed pen and paper and began to write to Johnny.

August 30, 2014

>I am so excited. I feel as if heaven has touched me, as if a neural soul way has been established—the opening of a passageway between you and me, as if sesame has opened and wonderful things are to come.

That event seemed to initiate a whole series of wondrous happenings. My frequent plaint that I did not feel Johnny's presence was silent for a time, for he had given me an unmistakable sign that he was with me. In the next two months, I felt his presence in a variety of new ways and was reminded of some old ways as well. In the space of little more than a month, I had two dreams in which I felt he had paid me a visit.

The first was a transcendent dream of joy. I was on our patio when I spotted several dolphins a ways up the lake heading toward me. I ran into the house calling for Johnny to come look, and he was there at once, excited to share with me this wonderful miracle as the dolphins frolicked before us. A little later, we lay on the bed together, talking and sharing another beautiful moment. I knew in the back of my mind that he would have to leave soon, but I felt so close to him and so joyful. I hadn't had a dream so delicious in many months.

The second began as an ordinary dream. The two of us were working on remodeling a house, and I left to get supplies. As I came back into the house, I heard him calling my name, and at that moment, I woke from the dream. As I awoke, I heard my name called, not in my mind, not in the dream, but I actually heard, with my physical ears, his voice calling, "Nita," and I started to answer but stopped myself, realizing he was not there. Then I remembered. Sometime in the week or two prior, I had heard him call me from another room in the middle of the night, and as I woke, I called out, "Yes?" When I realized he wasn't there, I went back to sleep and forgot about it. I wondered how often I had allowed his messages to fall back into my unconscious without ever examining them in the light of day.

And at last, I seemed able to sense his presence, often in meditation where he seemed to wrap his essence around me. Sometimes, I sensed the sweetness of his spirit, and at other times, his playful nature. Or nodding off for just a moment, I came to with the impression that we had been together. It seemed real—as if I had stepped away from this reality for the tiniest moment to a totally different place that was so sweet, so desirable that I wondered if I had been in the spirit world with him. These episodes were brief;

they seemed to happen in a split second. But they carried the flavor of such sweetness that I wanted to capture them forever.

And those lightning bolts that seemed to kick off this whole process? I continued to experience them frequently in meditation, not often as strong as they were that first time but consistently. I didn't know quite what to call them—vibrations, impulses, shocks? It was apparent that they came in response to my thoughts, so I learned not to go deep into hypnogogia during my meditations but to stay a little more on the surface, where I was aware of my musings. I wrote:

November 3, 2014

> These sensations are very pleasant, something I desire and seek to create, but I have absolutely no control over them. What do they mean? Do these impulses signal that something I am thinking is true? When does it happen? In moments when my self is aligning with your soul? In moments of love, or beauty, or truth? In moments when I am feeling joy deep within? And what of the day when I had the little "lightning storm" in my body for much of the meditation. I wasn't thinking or visualizing anything, just watching it happen and enjoying the sensation. I can't make it happen. It happens of its own accord, when I am least expecting it.

Then, in November, I came down with a bad cold that turned into bronchitis, and I was pretty much out of commission for nearly three weeks. During that time, although I continued to meditate, I fell out of communication with Johnny. I had no sensations that he was with me or any of the impulses that I had been puzzling over. But almost as soon as I was well, I began to feel his presence again. My soul ways were up and running. I had shared my experience of the lightning bolts with Jamie on a recent visit, and he agreed with my sense that those impulses—zings, he called them—were confirmations of a truth.

I could not read the energy. I longed for his words, for the soul of Johnny was poetry. In the messages I had received through mediums, he never failed to say that he loved me, but I missed the poetic images that he had used in communications with me in life—images of the moon, magnolias, midnight gardens, and things mysterious and magical. We had shared fantasies that we had been together through time in distant lands—in a garden of ancient Persia or beside a well in Damascus. Our visit to the Alhambra in Spain had moved us deeply. It called up ancient times with its Arabic history, Moorish architecture, and gardens filled with flower scents and sounds of water. And it was in the heart of Lorca's Andalucia. Lorca, himself, was captivated with images of Spain's Arabic past. In meditation, as I called up these images, which were accompanied by strong impulses, I had a growing sense that Johnny now existed in an Alhambra-like setting with lush gardens, where all the cats that had shared our lives were free to run.

Then one night I woke from a dream, in the darkest hours, deeply disturbed. Johnny had looked at me with sad eyes and said despairingly, "Everything is over." I tossed until morning, worrying and wondering, *Did he really speak to me? Was it reality or a fear-based dream?* As dawn broke, I remembered that the wonderful time during the day before, when I lunched with a friend, had been marred by a few words, which I had immediately forgotten in the buoyant mood of the moment. She had encouraged me to trust my experience and for the most part was validating about my connection with Johnny. But she said at one point that on my death, when I would meet him, that we might decide to go our separate ways. When I remembered this part of our conversation, it became clear to me from where the dream had arisen. She had tapped into my greatest fear of being without him forever.

As December deepened into dark days and long nights, I dreaded the coming of the new year that would mark two full years, 2013 and 2014, which he had never known. By the time the first day of January arrived, I was feeling lost and hopeless again. I had gone two lean weeks, during which I had heard nothing from him. Having sobbed much of the morning, I sat back in my chair and closed my eyes. I had not heard from him because I had been feeling dead inside. A line from a song started to play over and over in my mind, "The feeling's gone and I just can't get it back."

And I was thinking, *Yes, that's exactly it. I can't recreate the feeling.* Then I remembered a caution I had heard often—to pay attention when a song drops into the mind, as it may be a message from spirit. I keyed that line into my cell phone on the hunch that it was a song by Gordon Lightfoot. The lyrics appeared to "If You Could Read My Mind."

> Just like an old-time movie,
> 'Bout a ghost from a wishin' well
> In a castle dark or a fortress strong,
> With chains upon my feet.
> You know that ghost is me.
> And I will never be set free
> As long as I'm a ghost that you can't see.

I had no doubt that this was a message from Johnny. This verse was peppered with Romantic images that offered me assurance. But more important, he was reminding me that I had allowed myself to slip once again into a place where I could no longer feel his presence or see that he was truly with me. And even more than that, it proved to me that he wanted to be in contact as much as I did.

In the next verse, the singer speaks of himself as a failed hero in a book whose ending is so painful it could not be repeated. My last words to him as he passed were, "You're my hero." To repeat that ending would have been my greatest horror, even though it had played again and again in my mind, and I had experienced the agony of it a hundred times. He had, indeed, read my mind. How could I doubt that he was with me?

With a long sigh of relief and gratitude, I went to the patio door and looked out. A flotilla of coots, perhaps one hundred, was spread out across the water as they bobbed down the lake toward me. I had never seen so many. And the two hummingbirds, who were regulars at my feeder, chased through the tree and swooped down past my window. Nature was celebrating with me a beautiful message from Johnny. I said to him, "You have comforted my aching heart."

Three days later, my friend Neva called and told me she had dreamed about Johnny. He had said to her something that she didn't understand, "*Gacela* of unforeseen love," She said that she kept asking him in the dream, "Do you mean Giselle?" And finally, he spelled it out for her—G-a-c-e-l-a. She said it made no sense to her, but she woke up and wrote it down. It made no sense to me either. I was sitting in front of the computer as we spoke.

"I'll Google it," I told her. I typed in *gacela*, and before I could write it out, the phrase popped up, "Gacela of Unforeseen Love." I gasped. It was not just a fantastic dream pulled out of the air, as I suspected. It must mean something. I tapped "enter."

"*Gacela of Unforeseen Love by Federico Garcia Lorca,*" appeared on the screen. I literally lost my breath. Although Johnny had often shared with me translations of Lorca's poetry, I had never heard of a gacela. Yet I learned soon after that there were many in Lorca's collection of poems called *The Divan at Tamarit*. "Divan" is the term used for a group of poems in Persian or Arabic; it is said that Lorca used the term to evoke that ancient world.

The "Gacela of Unforeseen Love" is a dark poem to Lorca's lover that moves from a passionate moment to the acknowledgment of the separation death brings. And yes, the images dear to Johnny, the images I had longed for, were there: the moonlit garden in Andalucia, the magnolia, allusions to Persia, and a wish to declare undying love, which death inevitably steals. It was such a reminder of Johnny's intense passion as a participant in life, so reflective of my own secret longing for those many nights that we shared.

Neva emailed later that day that Johnny had given her a message for me that she had forgotten in the excitement of the moment of discovery. She had written it down when she awoke in the night to write the title of the *gacela*: "Anita, you are my soul mate, and I love you always. Always and so present." The words that he sent to me echoed the words in the poem:

> I sought in my heart to give you
> The ivory letters that say always,
> Always, always: garden of my agony,

As I sat down before bedtime, as was my custom, to read to him the events of the day I had recorded in my letter, the magnificence of the whole experience, the depth of the level of contact with him, impacted me fully: he had transmitted to me an echo of all our moments together, of the partings and reunions through time that we had shared, of the desire for eternal love overshadowed by the foreknowledge of death, the final parting. As I started to read, my whole body began to shake. My hands trembled, and my voice quavered so that I could hardly read the words. I was truly awestruck by a transcendent experience unlike anything I had known before. It had been a day of mystery upon mystery.

The messages of those early days in January left me feeling that he would share with me the sadness of our separation until we were once again fully together. They were even further validation that he and I had the same desire for this connection between earth and spirit. This remarkable experience was only the beginning of a re-blossoming of poetry and magic in my life.

Chapter 5

During the first days of January, I was consumed with thoughts of the "Gacela."

January 5, 2015

    The experience of the "Gacela" is pure magic—such an explicit and profound message, so full of your essence that I cannot doubt it. The message is filled with genius, filled with the spirit I know you to be. What an incredible thrill this has been, what an inspiriting adventure! I believe that the inspiration I have been seeking to write this book has been seeded in these recent hours I have spent with you—so near, so real. I feel the immediacy of your passion, of your presence, of your love; and whereas before, I have sensed your sweetness and your wit, this new sense of the intensity of your being brings you so close—almost as close as you were in life. The words of the "Gacela" are Lorca's, but your poetic spirit is carried on them to me.

I could not help but remark that the week before Neva had brought me the "Gacela," Janet had brought me a book containing poetry by Hafix, the Persian poet who created the gacela form, and she mentioned at the same time that she had run across the poem I had written the summer before, "Dancing with Lorca." As I looked back on this event, it seemed to be a prefiguring of the appearance of Lorca's "Gacela" and the inspiration that it brought me. Even at that moment, I was crafting another poem in my mind.

On January 10, I was stricken with another bout of flu, ending with bronchitis and lasting a month, a twin of the first. My meditations during this time were especially intense. I continued to puzzle over the meaning of those impulses I was feeling throughout my body. I, at last, concluded that this was a sign of his presence, which would come to me when I was focusing on those ideas that were significant in our relationship—ideas that resonated with both of us and set up an energetic communication. I could feel this energy zinging throughout my body, his light dancing at the top of my head. It was a most beautiful and intimate feeling.

Since I felt like going nowhere, doing nothing, it gave me opportunity to process the meaning of the miracle of the new year, and although I did no writing at the time, the idea of my new poem began to take shape. In the Lightfoot song was a message. I was failing to see the obvious signals Johnny was sending that he was constantly with me. From the ghost's message, that he will never be free until he can be seen, I surmised that Johnny must be telling me he could not take advantage of the freedom his new life offered him until I acknowledged those intimations of his presence. Now I accepted the "Gacela" as irrefutable evidence that he was with me. It allowed me, at last, to see him clearly in my mind's eye.

The image that Johnny existed in a place resembling the Alhambra had been fresh in my mind when the Lorca poem, set in a Granada garden, had spoken powerfully to that notion. And in that clearer vision, I sensed he had changed—with his full magnificence shining through with even greater wisdom and love than he had in life. I wanted to assure him that I knew he was with me.

Alhambra

I see you now
Yet walk alone
Along this twilight path.

A phantom figure,
Mist beyond lattice,
Forms and dissolves.
And candle drifts
Along the arches,
Glimpsed, then gone.
A shimmering wing,
Invisible yet seen.

And you to me,
Ephemeral but real,
Echoing Lorca
In the fading light.

Right after I completed this poem, I received an urge, in meditation, to go to a book that I knew had been on our library shelf for many years, *Andalucia & Garcia Lorca*, ostensibly to find pictures of the Alhambra to show to Janet. As I was looking over the book, I noticed at the back, tucked into the flyleaf, a long envelope. Nothing was written on the outside, and, curious, I pulled from it a single, folded sheet of onionskin typing paper. I carefully opened it out and found within a large yellow leaf, still pliant, fresh, as if it had just fallen from the tree. Printed on the leaf, in ink, were the words "I Love You." I saw immediately that the letter was written in the very distinctive italics font of the typewriter that had been in Johnny's office at ASU. It had to have been written before 1992, the year that he retired and left the typewriter behind, and it brought to mind a familiar fantasy he had loved to spin that we were children together.

And one day, when they were children, (when were they not?) he followed her down a narrow path that led to the magnolia tree—and she stopped suddenly, and knelt down to examine a yellow leaf that had just spiralled down beside her—and there was something in the way she touched the leaf that touched something inside him, and he reached his right hand and lightly touched her hair, to be for a moment a part of this beautiful thing—she brushed her hair lightly, thinking (as she probably still does) that it was a butterfly—
And years later she asked him "what is it like to love me?"
And he knew that it had to do with sensations of connections—
And he looked at a yellow leaf, and read his fortune in its first-day-of fallness, and its lines were like the lines in his hand—and he was that leaf, and he knew what it was to be connected to a branch,
and the branch to a trunk,
and the trunk to roots,
and the roots to the earth
And loving her was hearing her heart beat, which connected him to the beating of the universe,
For the most beautiful part of him had come into existence in her womb,
floating on a warm sea
And the pounding of her heart,
in the chamber above him
moved him as he had not been moved.
And loving her was being joined to every beautiful thing in the universe, just as he had felt on that day so long ago so near when she knelt on the path and held a leaf in her hand...
And no matter how much separation they may share, when they die, they will find inside each of them, a tiny golden room,
Shining in its golden splendor, and
Totally intact.   J.

I was overcome by a welling of emotion—joy, nostalgia, and, yes, grief at the loss of a companion whose words were golden. I knew he had directed me here to find this letter that had lain hidden for at least twenty-five years. The message was so poignant, so particular to my sadness of the moment, a promise that we would be together again, our love intact, and the leaf as fresh as our love promised to be when we would at last reunite. It stirred memories of the cards and letters he had given me over a period when we had experienced many times apart; these were messages I had tucked into a shoebox. They had remained unexamined for as many years as this letter had rested within the flyleaf of *Andalucia y Garcia Lorca*.

The box had been residing at the far corners of my mind ever since he had been gone, but I had only once lifted the lid—the day I discovered a birthday card from him standing beside it. I had looked only at the top card from our son Sean. Now I was certain that beneath that card were the precious memories I had stored away. I climbed the stairs and sidled my way into the back of a closet to pull open the drawer of a file cabinet and remove the box. I lifted the lid and cautiously peeked beneath the card from Sean. There it was—the shoebox stuffed with cards and letters, my name enscribed on the envelopes in Johnny's familiar hand.

I was so hungry for his words, I began to dig through the box, clutching at its contents, scanning voraciously poems penned on elaborate greeting cards or simply typed on index cards or onionskin paper. The box was filled with poetry he had given me over the years and letters he had sent me during his stays in Spain. Suddenly I stopped, realizing this was not a meal to be consumed in one sitting but a gift to be savored, slowly, deliciously. The letters were written on the fragile airmail paper of the time, and the poetry on carefully selected cards, bearing romantic images that often recalled those youthful dreams we had shared of the Arabian nights and Persian gardens. The dried delicate flowers that had been pressed within them wanted to crumble as I touched them. I began to collect the cards that I had strewn around me on the floor where I sat and carefully returned each card to its place in the stack. Most were undated, and I wished to keep some sense of continuity, to place them in time. I was able to determine from dates on the letters and a few of the cards that these were given to me through the 1980s, but it was not long before I realized that they were timeless. The opening of the box gave rise to a new aspect of communication between us.

At the end of the day, overwhelmed with emotion, I wrote in my nightly letter:

February 25, 2015

> My beloved, I ache so for your touch, your presence, your comfort. I want so to be with you—in that place where all is love. I thought, when I sought out the box today, with your cards, letters, notes to me, that I could take delight in the poetry of your words—and oh, yes, I did, but also, they pierced the place in my heart that longs so deeply for the fullness of your presence, and they brought forth a flood of tears. I read of times when I was away, and you were home missing me, and times when you were far off in Spain, longing for communication, carefully outlining the particular moments that you would be in a place where I could call. How lonely those times were for both of us. But there was always the assurance that we would be together again.
>
> Yet not so anymore. Here, there were no assurances, only faith and hope. But the knowledge that I could go to the box to find words of encouragment buoyed my spirits. I wanted to reserve the cards for future times when I would need their support. I wished to read them one by one, linger over them, savoring each word. And finally, I would bring them, one at a time, to share with Janet. The first one that I took to her quoted lines from a verse of the *Rubaiyat* that I had loved so much as a girl and had shared with him the first days of our meeting:

> Ah love! could thou and I with Fate conspire
> To grasp this sorry Scheme of Things entire,
> Would we not shatter it to bits—and then
> Re-mould it nearer to the Heart's Desire!

And inside, he had written simply,

Perhaps we have.   Love, J.

Those three words spoke volumes to me. They called up a whole lifetime of sharing poetry and realizing our dreams, and the immense good fortune we had in being together. And they offered me a whole new concept to contemplate and delight in. Had we, indeed, conspired with fate, in some far-off world, to make this magic happen? I believed we had. And he, perhaps, believed it too.

I continued to waver between two states of being—the depression created by my longing for his physical presence and the delight of this new connection. In meditation, I could feel his energy moving through my body and believe fully that we were together in spirit—that we were creating a new relationship, which would ultimately be better than the one we had before. I no longer had to rely on Jamie to bring me, imperfectly, the sense of who he was. This box, which had become a magical tool for me, had given me tangible evidence that he was as I remembered him—I could read his words and respond to them. Although I had remembered that he had given me beautiful messages, almost every detail of what he had written had gone from my mind. The terror I had experienced through the months he had been gone was that I would forget who he was. But now I realized that I might forget days we spent together, words we spoke to each other, but I would never forget the essence of his being. Strangely, there was only one of his verses that I remembered, and I had dug through the box when I first opened it to find it. He knew of my desire (never realized) to have a white Corvette.

> *To Anita, Driving by in a White Corvette*
> *At first I thought it was a low-flying white cloud*
> *Scudding, perhaps—with dark edges,*
> *But there it was,*
> *Its tinted rear window past me before it was ever*
> *alongside me,*
> *And I wouldn't have known it was her,*
> *Except for the way the palm trees shone in the sun*
> *As she passed under them,*
> *On her way to the Superstitions,*
> *On her way to my heart.*

Somehow, that poem had fulfilled my desire. Never again did I long for a white Corvette.
I wrote to him soon after …

March 2, 2015

That box of memories brings the recollection of such joy, but the reminder of the loss of it is so painful. The skies are heavy today with dark clouds, which are a reflection of my soul—longing for you, tangled in a net of past and future—remembering and hoping. The box, full of you, draws me, charms me. I want to return to it again and again, hug it to me, love it as if it were you. The small rain has rained all day, and I think of those lines.

> Western wind when wilt thou blow
> The small rain down can rain
> Christ if my love were in my arms
> And I in my bed again.[5]

---

[5] Words from a sixteenth-century Middle English song, given here in modern English.

Lessons in Poetry

My life has been about loving you, and it always will be. So what is left for me, knowing this as fact? To write about you, how I love you, how you love me, and what a perfect thing this is.

March 5, 2015, set record highs all over the Southwest, and Phoenix was no exception, with thermometers hovering near one hundred, a jarring leap in temperature, which even desert dwellers are unaccustomed to. On that day, I was headed out for a long-awaited meeting with a spiritual counselor named Hilary. Half an hour before I was to leave, I experienced the auras that presage a migraine headache. Trying to ignore the pain, I set out, determined not to miss this engagement and praying this would be one of my lesser episodes. My destination was accessed by a narrow route that led up a mountain and off onto a side street near the summit. It was a good distance from where I lived in the suburbs, and when I headed my car up the mountain, I was relieved to see that I had given myself plenty of time. Suddenly, I came upon a blockade that allowed no further access. I turned back to try another route but found, after several such attempts, every avenue to my destination blockaded for street paving. Finally, I put a call in to Hilary, who cheerfully offered to walk down and meet me at the blockade. I pulled over and got out of the car, with a throbbing head, to blistering heat and blinding sun and began trudging up the mountain toward the blockade. I was beginning to view this as a symbolic journey, a test of my resolve.

Hilary asked me inside, and as we settled in, I told her my situation as a widow of two years who seemed to be marking time as I looked forward to joining my husband. And soon, she began a reading that was to alter completely the perception I held of my life, so absorbing that, after a few minutes, I didn't notice that my headache had vanished.

Almost at once, Hilary told me, "There is a search you've been on this lifetime to become complete, that would have you feel fulfilled, and I sense that it's been elusive. You can tell me whether it's true or not."

My response was uncalculated. I may even have been a bit surprised at why I answered as I did. Yet in retrospect, I understand it was exactly what I needed to say. "It's been like my quest for the holy grail. In fact, my favorite fairy tale, when I was little, was *Rumpty Dudget's Tower*, about a little girl who had three tasks to complete. I see how that has kind of run my life."

She asked to know more about the tale, and I recounted the narrative for her, to which she responded, "It was as if you have to go to the heights and the depths before you can live in balance and bring harmony to your life. You felt that it was your sacred mission to restore the garden to its sacred order, interweaving all the routes—the underworld, the infinite route. I would say this is a metaphor that spoke to what your earth journey is about. I'm validating for you that this is not some silly story. This is a beautiful metaphor that was given to you, which you have held like a jewel in your heart, and there's truth to it."

She said of me then, "You've had a wide-eyed, innocent search in your life. Regardless of whatever years you've had attached to your name, you've actually had the eyes of the innocent child throughout your whole life, that ability to look with the eyes of a child that sees magic, that sees things afresh, that is able to be in awe and wonderment."

She spoke of Johnny as well. "He was really holding that little girl and gave her a way to be in the world that was safe and protected, cared for and cherished. What you gave him was a part of himself that he was not in touch with—that ability to see with innocent eyes, the eyes of truth, of love, of awe and wonderment. The two of you had this beautiful agreement to experience the world together, using your eyes on the world, his ability to dream and interpret. The two of you were able to travel together in your lives and experience many things from this beautiful place."

I agreed with her, shared with her how I had found the letter in the book and later discovered the box of his writings—how he spoke of the two of us as children together.

Hilary went on. "It was an otherworldly world that you got to inhabit, and without him here, it's hard for you to inhabit it, because he was part of creating and holding it."

There was much more, but I couldn't wait to ask her about the book. I told her that Janet had suggested over a year ago that I write a memoir honoring his life and that recently I had been giving it serious consideration. But I acknowledged that it was also a huge commitment for me to take on so late in life. Yet it would fulfill my wish to write a tribute to him.

And then we both expressed the idea, almost in the same breath, that this would be a weaving of his poems and mine. "And maybe," she continued, "your book is a way of having him be seen and to bring his essence, which is still left here in the world in his poetry. What if he's watching over you so you can bring that piece, which has sense in another realm and is not yet brought into this realm, and as you bring it through, you're not completing just your life, but you are completing both your lives?"

Yes, I thought, *what if…*

What a beautiful concept that was. In that moment, she gave me a sense of purpose about the book, that it would complete our relationship on this earth and that whether or not I ever shared it with anyone, the writing of it was the important thing.

"He will help you with this," she told me as we parted. "He already has."

The day had been mythic for me—from the labyrinthine journey up the mountain, facing dead ends at every turn, to the meeting of a wise woman who pulled random threads from my consciousness and wove them into a beautiful tapestry. She fit all the intimations floating in my psyche into the allegory I had chosen for my life and, finally, was instrumental in sealing it with the reemergence of a long-lost story. She had allowed me to see the archetypes that were playing out in my life.

Over the next days, my excitement about writing the story of Johnny and me continued to grow. It was the story of the journey of our lives, which had come to fruition in the full realization of our love, only after we had experienced the final separation. I believed, as I would write and he would guide my hand, it was up to us together to bring this story into words, whether published or tucked away, which would be the evidence that it happened, that it was real, and that it was magic.

I had opened the box on February 25, 2015, and ten days later, I visited Hilary. I did not note at the time the synchronicity of these two events, nor was I aware of the impact they would have on my life and my vision.

And then I had a dream. I dreamed of Eurydice, a white Persian cat, a favorite of mine and a dear friend. She died in 1980. I dreamed that in spite of a promise to her that she would be with me always, I had given her away. I was inconsolable and wanted to get her back, but I couldn't remember where she was. I was frantic, desperate to find the name of the person who had her, looking through shoeboxes and cabinets for the name, and I awoke deeply depressed. The dream had caused deep feelings of guilt to resurface. Ever since Eurydice died in 1980, I felt I had betrayed her by not being by her side when she died. I easily could have been, but I chose not to. I had sought redemption through the years by giving exquisite attention to the cats in my care, but I continued to carry the guilt of that betrayal.

I saw at once what had precipitated that dream. For in the meeting with Hilary, there was a dark spot that I had chosen to ignore. When I told her of the months I had spent reviewing my life with Johnny after he was gone, she cautioned me I would find times, in my visits to the box, that I would be thrown back into difficult moments where I would castigate myself for behaving as I did. "This will be an opportunity," she told me, "for you to bring absolute love to yourself. Your doing that will put you in a place where you will be ready to die in peace and surrender and gratitude, with no regrets." She told me that, according to the different traditions, that is the state we aim for at the end of life and that many say you don't need to come back if you have achieved it.

I knew that I did not want to return to the cycle of life on earth, and I also knew that I was a long way from loving myself, from forgiving myself. Janet had for two years gently cajoled me not to be so hard on myself, but self-flagellation is a habit that's hard to give up. Because I knew what a difficult taskmaster my inner critic was, I didn't know how I would ever learn to love myself. I sat with this dark mood until I saw Janet again. She showed me how the rules I had set for my life had prevented me from being with Eurydice, how that option was not even open to me at the time. I could see she had a point. And I felt deeply that as I let go of the judgments I had on myself, I would come closer to actually "seeing" Johnny—that there would come a time when I could be with him in an even more connected way.

Hilary had said something else that stuck in my mind. "The two of you are woven together like DNA. That's not gone away. It's just that one of you is in one world, and one in the other. You're in both worlds, and he's in both worlds, and yet you are predominantly here, and he's predominantly there." I found that concept inspiring, and the first lines of a poem about it came in meditation, as they were wont to do. In three days, the poem had seemed to complete itself.

DNA

> What other worlds
> Do you inhabit,
> While I am left
> With ragged traces
> Of a magic life?
> Do you dance in a cosmos of light?
> As I weep in a valley of shadow,
> Your dream a palette of brilliance,
> My vision dull, muted by tears.

> But listening,
> I hear whispers of worlds combined.
> Sun-Moon are one,
> Soul strands entwined,
> Mirrors reversed,
> Loves unreflecting,
> Blending seen and unseen,
> Merging now and always,
> Death an illusion.

That night I wrote to him:

March 19, 2015

    This poem is an assertion that we are together, even though I feel apart from you. I wish I could feel the togetherness. I believe it. I know deep in my soul that we have a magic, a love that will sustain us—that one day, in another world, this truth will become evident. And that said, in this place of flesh and bone, where the sun sets and the moon rises, I miss you. I cry to hear your voice and feel your presence.

Chapter 6

The rediscovery of the box was a remarkable event for me, and after that first rush to find what he had written, I decided on a more cautious approach. This gift, I recognized, had limits, and I wanted to savor it as long as I could. Although I continued to pull the cards from the box, I parceled them out, waiting a week, sometimes much longer, before reaching for the next. And I lingered over each one, bringing it forth each day and reading it again and again. I had written him each night for nearly a year, yet the opening of the box had given rise to a new aspect of communication between us. For now, I was receiving messages as well as sending them to him. In a magical way, his writings often seemed to make connection with something that was going on in my own experience. In a letter sent from the island of Gomera, he tells of his vision of us resting in a cornfield. He scoops a handful of earth and allows it to sift through his fingers, inscribing the letters "I love you" from my left foot to my left shoulder. And I wondered about those thrills I was getting in meditation that coursed through my body in exactly that way—from my left foot to my left shoulder. Was he sending me that very message of love?

As I read his writings, I berated myself for giving so little attention to these poems when I first received them in the eighties, remembering how I had read them and put them aside with casual thanks. I was appalled by my lack of understanding and appreciation. I told him in my nightly messages how I was seeing, for the first time, the depth of his insight into our soul connection. And the frequent envisioning of that connection, stretching back into an imagined childhood, continued to surface in his writings:

> *And he remembered another time and place, a small town in the south, the middle of a long summer—we are children of seven, live on the same street—dusty once-white houses, each with a porch the length of the house, each with a swing. Wooden unpainted fences enclose beds of iris, many with magnolia trees in front—a man in a white shirt holds a hose in his right hand, watering the iris. He has removed his flannel hat with his left hand, and holds the hat as he wipes the sweat from his forehead with his left arm. The heat is all pervasive, the topic of every conversation—a neighbor leans on the fence and observes, "She's gonna be a scorcher," which is evident even at nine in the morning. And it is a joyful time for us—the heat enters every pore of the morning. That and the length of the day give a kind of epic background to the summer, and it is as if we have become the heat itself, lying under a willow watching a mocking bird open and close its wings.*
>
> *And the days have a heartbeat and pulse, made up of banging screendoors, the rustle of paper fans—some say,"Drink RC cola"—the squeaking of the front porch swing, the calls of parents at nightfall that interrupt the daily hide-and-go-seek games. And sometimes we hide together, and once I pretended to fall asleep, and I felt your breath and your eyelashes on my cheek and then your lips. I will never know how you didn't know that every atom in my body was whirling like a dust devil. And whenever we walked on different sides of a tree or telephone pole, one of us would say bread and butter, and that's how we were, like warm butter melting into every pore of the bread.*

And in the evening love entered and left and entered again, with the flies, thru the holes in the screen door, and I would push you in the swing, and, sometimes, you seemed suspended in the swing, above the low-rising moon and stars. At times, I believe that my whole life has passed while I waited for the swing to return, and I wouldn't be surprised to find myself on that porch, about to send you off on another voyage to the stars.

And one day a man in a dark blue suit and a woman in a white dress, with a picture hat with daisies all around the crown, entered one of the houses—I don't know if yours or mine—and we followed them, since they seemed to suggest exciting possibilities. We followed dark suit and daisy hat into the cool-damp parlor, and a shadowy figure pulled up the shade a bit, allowing a pure shaft of sunlight to enter—light filled with thousands of gyrating specks of dust, as your eyes sometimes fill with golden specks of love.

And you and I—behind a sofa covered with red roses, each restsing one elbow on the sofa's wooden frame, cupping chin in hand—watch dark suit and daisy hat, and another unclear figure. And we somehow knew that the whispered words they murmered would affect us, and I felt your hand touch mine—and a blue jay passed the window. Daisy Hat would sometimes move her head, indicating that one of us figured in the conversation, and it was a tiny theatre, not a parlor, and we were characters in the play.

And we knew we would be separated, or, at least, would seem to be separated, but could they, planning our lives, possibly know that to separate you from me would be like separating the green from the brown on that single leaf that we found one day in the magic woods we loved so much?

(Here a leaf is taped, now dry.)

> *And could they know that one day we discovered that our hearts were interchangeable, and that sometimes we would reach inside our shirts at the same time, and I would throw you my heart, and you would throw me yours, and they would not miss a beat ...*
> *And could they know that I loved you then, already, As I love you now.*

March 22, 2015

You write with an awareness of the time when we would be permanently separated, yet you had the vision, even then, that nothing could separate us—we would always be a part of each other. It is as if there was intention in your words, even then, to comfort me in this time when I am so in need of comfort. Almost every flower, every leaf, that you enclosed in those beautiful gifts to me remains—dried, but still with me. I can live with no other reality than you are here with me now, and I am there with you. Let that be enfolded in my dreams and in my mind until I feel it, know it with a certainty beyond life and death.

In the midst of the intensity of the lessons I was gleaning from his poetry, I had lunch with a woman who had been a student of Johnny's. She spoke of how she had not understood poetry before she took his class and how he had opened a whole new world to her. She ended by saying, "I love your husband." There were many who loved him because they recognized in him the soul of a poet. He touched lives with his intense feeling for Lorca's poetry and with his own "duende." So did I express my love in my nightly musings to him.

March 27, 2015

And I love you for every bit of who and what you are—the

Lessons in Poetry

madman and the genius, the rebel and the poet, the actor and the lover. I love your words. I love your physical form that lay beside me through ten thousand nights and your spirit so full of laughter and joy. Thank you for being with me through your poetry, like the one I found today.

Weekend Without You

Friday, 4:30 pm—I walk to the French doors, look onto the screened porch, and a single strand of a spider's web, surrounded by light, extends from the door to a creosote bush. And I see, on the bush, drops of rain—globes of fire, and the single strand is you—me and it is so strong, and it is so vulnerable to breaking, and I feel your presence, so strong, and yet I dare not open the door.

Saturday, 1:00 pm—looking through the book of unicorns—tiny winged creatures decorate a unicorn with flowers, and my thoughts, now sticky-winged, rush back to another time and place, and you and I are children in the same small town—and now you are seated, legs extended, in a red wagon that says American Coaster on the side, and there is to be a children's parade, and I will pull you in the wagon and now I kneel beside the wagon and tie lilacs and daisies in your hair and to your arms, and as I kneel there I do not understand the words that crouch on my tongue—I love you mommy, don't ever die.

Saturday, 5:00 pm—a pure ray of sunlight enters the narrow west window of the living room, confusing shadows of bamboo and flamingo legs filled with microscopic butterflies, and I wish you were here, and we would hold crystals and candles in the light, and I follow the ray of light into the past, and now, in the woods we so often played in as children, I have discovered a great shaft of light, passing diagonally thru a magnolia tree, and I know what I must do—first, to Hobson's Mercantile Store, where I have been fascinated by a display of crystals and pieces of glass—offering to sweep out the store if they will let me borrow the display for only half an hour. I run with the glittering treasure, hidden in a bag, to your house. "Come and find me in the woods," I shout to you. A quick stop at my house to gather up all the belts and rope I can find, then to the woods and the great beam of light, brighter than ever. Now, I tie dozens of crystals and pieces of glass, mostly blue, with belts and rope, to my body—now I hear your steps down the path. I feel my heart beating with your steps—

And there he is—this spindly-legged Prometheus, arms extended, offering the gift of fire to man, offering his love, in each embryonic rainbow, to you.

J.

I found the image of the child Prometheus so touching that I felt moved to respond to it, but I could not find the words, nor grasp the concept of the poem I wished to write. I was getting fragments of it in meditation—inspired by him, I was certain. Struggling for days to articulate what I was feeling, I asked him:

March 31, 2015

Where are you leading me, my beloved muse? Perhaps I am carrying your inspiration but without your eloquence to cause it to bloom. Do I remain here to learn what you already knew? If what I have imagined is true—that the transformation that happens in the process of being here and connecting with you across time and space is the seal that joins us forever—then I am willing to be here. I am willing to suffer the loneliness without you, the loss of your physical form, the empty days and nights that are required of me in order to spend eternity with you. Perhaps I have come to the point of surrender—yet even this has conditions.

Still, I could not let go of my enchantment with the youthful fire bringer of his fantasy. At last, I managed these few lines:

Soul Fire

To what purpose
My life here?
Trapped in an earth-bound vision
That splits all things apart.
(Sesame!
Where is the crack between the worlds,
That I might slip away and be with him?)

I reach for you,
Stretching my arms into the void,
Blindly seeking
To touch your soul.

Our souls combine
And kindle stars
To silent flame,
Which seals forever after
The pact we made on earth.
And in their midst,
Within their glow,
You, Prometheus dancing,
Have lit eternal fire within my heart.

My sense of a mystical connection continued to grow as I read more of his poetry and sent my responses in letters to him. It was as if the thirty or more years since he had created those poems had vanished, and we were leaving love notes for each other day by day, just as he had left those messages for me in the distant past. I was understanding for the first time the meaning of a love that bonded two souls together no matter how far apart they might seem in time or space. I could see how such wisdom had passed me by when I had read his poetry the first time, and only now was I beginning to learn it.

April 11, 2015

A line in the first letter I found from you that speaks of how loving me had to do with sensations of connections is a powerful one. The sensations I receive from you in meditation are the continuing proof of the connection we have and the love we hold for each other. Feeling your energy course through me is as powerful as the grief that plagues me. But the energy comes suddenly and leaves quickly. It doesn't have that quality of duration that the anguish has. I wish I could learn to hold the feeling in the way I am so good at holding the grief. You have come to me in such amazing ways, yet I am in constant battle not to slip into the well of deep sadness at your absence.

Occasionally, not even every weekend, I would take another card gently from the box, open it carefully to save any fragment of a leaf or a flower that might be preserved within, and read his words.

And I have encountered you across the centuries
At a well, on the road to Damascus,
In a walled garden, in Bagdad.
Thank you for a thousand and one gifts of your beauty.
You are the shadow of a white rose on the grass,

A red seed on a white petal,
A candle's flame on a snowflake,
Something of you is in everything I seek,
And everything that eludes me.
And while you live,
I shall love no other,
As I love you.
				J.

May 7, 2015

Much as I love your poetry, it does not always have the power to lift me out of sadness. I wish so much that I could rejoice in every moment of our eternal connection and in the beauty of your words, the love that you express. Would that I could always have a sense that we are together, even though we live in two worlds. Yet these ideas now pale beside the memory of your arms around me through the night, your occasional touch through the day. Such thoughts leave a great void in the center of my being.

This was one of the many times when emptiness overtook me completely, so that my soul seemed frozen in an icy wasteland, a place so familiar that I had given it a name—The Dead Zone. When I was in that space, I could feel neither loved nor loving. Not even when Neva sent me a Mother's Day gift, a tiny silver heart suspended on a delicate chain looped through an infinity symbol. She told me of a dream in which Johnny had asked her to include the symbol of eternity from him. She had already proven to me that she had a true dream connection with him, yet what ordinarily would have moved me to tears failed to stir my heart. Realizing that the awe and wonder with which I had received the "Gacela" was missing from that moment, I mourned my failure of faith in our love and our connection. I felt helpless to do anything but wait for some synchronicity to happen, for a word from him that would stir my soul. Yet I resisted going to the box. Perhaps it was the fear of feeling sadness.

When I could no longer tolerate The Dead Zone, the place without love, the land of no feeling of any kind, I returned to the box, hoping to be rewarded.

> *The afternoon stretched out on a hammock, one end tied to that place in my neck where anxiety has been known to hang out, the other end tied to the horizon. And I held my hand in front of the sun, and its veins and lines became the veins and lines of a leaf—and I said hello to my mortality, and wondered if anyone had seen me or heard me—and I wished to leave a shadow of my hand, reaching toward someone I love, the echo of a word of mine, trapped between the petals of a rose.*
>
> *And then I thought of you, My Love, and how you saw me and how you heard me—and the dry leaves were magically sewn together, and their roughness became the smoothness of a magic cloak—and I knew your love once more.*
>
> *J.*

May 30, 2015

Today, your card released my frozen heart, melted it with a flood of tears. Although the reason I do not return to the box more often is to avoid the pain, I need to learn over and over again that avoiding the pain is more miserable than allowing myself to feel it. And the synchronicity of this moment is clear to me, how our separate lines of poetry, created so many years apart, echo each other. Look how alike they are! It is as if you cast a wish into the ether—

Lessons in Poetry

*I wished to leave a shadow of my hand,
reaching toward someone I love,*

*The echo of a word of mine, trapped between the
petals of a rose.*

And I sent the message back in some hastily scribbled lines that are still waiting for a poem to attach to:

I find your echoes,
Unfaded by the years,
Like fresh-dropped petals strewn along the path of time.

You asked; I answered. Yet my answer had been written some time before I read the question. Is this not magic? It seems as if our voices are echoing each other, sounding through the years that separate us from a time when our love was earthbound. Your words express a separation that is banished by reconnecting with a love that melts the heart. There was such love released with my tears on reading this poem, such relief from the loneliness that numbness creates. Perhaps I can learn to stop avoiding grief, knowing that it brings lost feelings to the surface to be experienced again, and those feelings are filled with love. Thank you for this card. It has broken me from silence and cracked the protective shell around my heart. Without communication from you, I am without inspiration.

In response to those feelings, these lines came to me at various times: while drifting off to sleep, at the end of meditation, or driving along the freeway. I could not distinguish whether he or I was writing them.

Echoes

Through labyrinthine canyons of the years,
The distance grows since then
But cannot still the echoes
That travel then to now and back again
And meet and merge
In shadowy euphony.

Days of our youth
In a more real canyon,
One in which the lost can be regained,
Where echoed laughter
Slides along the lizard's back,
Vibrates the manzanita,
Reverberates among stone phantoms,
Until,
Caught beside the torrent's flood,
Another inch
We could have died together.

This stony emptiness within
That knows no love,
You melt it with a word.
The images you offer,
Fresh yet familiar,
Haunt like an air
That soul once sang.
And am I voicing thoughts of yours,
Or are you speaking me?

June 18, 2015

Do you know how deeply you are seen and heard? If I failed to respond to your poetry in the way you might have hoped during those days of long ago, please know how deeply it moves me now.

Soon after, as I sat on the patio in early morning to catch the last gasp of coolness on a hot, mid-June day, a monarch butterfly swept across my line of vision. I felt Johnny with me. Later that day, I visited the box again. As was my custom, I took the card lying on top. Should I have been surprised, as I drew the card from its envelope, to find it was entitled "Butterfly"?

> *And when depression's night comes to the gardens within me and my insides hang down like broken branches, the shining butterfly of your love flutters thru my stomach, across my heart like Slide Rock, out my mouth, and perches on the end of my pen—balancing like a bird landing on a branch. And now the butterfly begins to move the pen—I love you. You are a precious creature.   J.*

It became more and more apparent to me that these messages written to me in the eighties were not at all for that time, when he was right there with me, but they were written to me for this present moment. Somehow, he had reached through the veil that clouds our eyes to draw from eternity the words that one day would bring the reality of his presence to my lonely heart. I had been reading Anita Moorjani's memoir, *Dying to Be Me*, which illustrated that every moment of eternity is happening in the ever-present now. Eternity is always here, at our fingertips. It is often touched in poetry. Thus, my heartache was calmed, and I found peace within his words for a few days, maybe a week.

But then, again, the fear rose into my throat, the skeptic hammered at my thoughts, until I cried out to him, "I am so aching to hear from you. Can you please send me a message?" He never seemed to lose patience with me. Two nights later, I was propped up in bed reading the last pages of Moorjani's book. I was startled by a loud whisper that spoke my name—Anita. I was certain it came from him. I could have marked the spot in the room where the whisper originated—just beyond the foot of the bed and to the right two feet. So near! I went to sleep feeling close to him once more.

I continued to ride these peaks and valleys, even though I felt his presence almost daily in meditation.

July 6, 2015

I feel, in your vibrations, that these moments are times when I transcend this world and, however briefly, am with you—with beauty, with goodness. And that this is a particular blessing that has been given me through you. The days that I begin with a meditation where you are present are better days for me because, through these, your presence in my life is constantly renewed. There are times that I feel I can be satisfied that our relationship is long distance. There is not the lovely intimacy of being held and holding you, but I feel our love has deepened and expanded.

I mused through a number of days about how we had mirrored each other in life. How, even though the only mirror I had reflected back to me an aging woman, I felt beautiful because he, as my mirror, saw beauty in me. And again, he echoed the theme of my thoughts:

And the birds listen for your heartbeat
So that they can adjust their being to your beauty—
And the iris seek their blue in your eyes,
And the breeze does not know if it is rippling through
Your hair or the flower—
And the moon is full
Of love for you,
As I am

And when we are not together
Pieces of my insides
Hang down like broken guitar strings,
But I still hear the echo of your love,
As your reflection lives in me. J.

July 8, 2015

And does our love not carry the potential to be all things to each other? Parent, child, brother, sister, being together in all seasons of life, as children, as lovers, as bosom companions, and, at last, reflecting our images so fully that we become each other.

He wrote:

And the velvet evening
Rubbed against him like a cat asking to be fed,
And the evening arched its back
And became the moon,
With a curved icicle
Clinging to its darkness.
Or was it the other side of a tapestry, or
The negative of some cosmic photograph?
And her dark-slivered hand
Cupped her white breast
And offered it to her child-lover

And he reached to the [branch],
Pulled off an exclamation mark,
So that he could tell her
I LOVE YOU!
(The exclamation point is made of twig and berry)

July 10, 2015

And are we now living on two sides of that tapestry, you on one side, I on the other, weaving ourselves together with our words?

And so I drifted through the summer, ignoring health concerns, caught up in reading his poetry and responding to it as the season continued to yield a rich store of his words. I carried him in my heart throughout the day: in my musings on my walk, listening to the chatter of birds in the freshness of the predawn morning, remembering how he loved even the tiniest flower. I would appreciate along my way the orange and yellow bursts of the Mexican bird of paradise, the intense red of the bougainvillea, and the plump bellies of the developing fruit of the pomegranate bush. Or when I returned to my patio to refresh the hummingbird feeder, I saw his greeting in the salute of the hummingbird as it hovered a foot from my nose and looked me square in the eye for long seconds, allowing me a glimpse of the startling scarlet patch on its throat. Or as I spoke with a friend over lunch about my desire to write, I imagined he spoke to me as I broke open a fortune cookie and read, "You have a way with words and should write a book." And his own way with words was ever with me:

> And sometimes my heart is like a budding plant—
> Bursting with love for you
> And our shining moments together—
> Streams where there are no streams,
> Birds feeding from your hand—
> Angel sister's bursting tomb and blue dragon flies,
>   fluttering—perhaps—back to life.
> And at times I feel like your sweet-faced, tattle-tale brother,
> Blind from birth,
> And you interpret the world for me,
> And at times we leave together,
> And no one can find us
> And even our mother

Could not tell us apart—
Only the stars,
Clustered about us,
Watching you,
A painted creature,
Crouched in my painted heart.
J.

July 12, 2015

Thank you for this beautiful poem, which reaches across the years and whispers to me that it is not a product of your life here but something plucked from eternity. It is the juxtaposition of the cycle of life and rebirth and the stillness of perfection that our love encompasses. Our relationship has grown to mystical proportions, and I find in your spirit the love—the moments of transcendence—that others find in their religion. To be a part of your sweet soul is all I could ask of eternity.

Toward the end of July, I was at last pushed to turn my thoughts to other matters. I had visited my doctor two months before and had failed to mention to him troubling symptoms, which continued to persist. I could ignore them no longer. When I saw him again, I was sent at once to a specialist who ordered a uterine MRI. And even as I came home and read another card from the box, I failed to connect the dark atmosphere of the card with my own situation. My response was one of joy.

And when he received the engraved invitation to attend a pre-concert recital of Mister Death and His One-Man-Band, he went directly to the designated basement dungeon of the old castle—and the recital had already begun. Mister Death was clanging a garbage can lid with the rusty spike from a railroad that no longer ran between Granada and Alicante. As a waiter led him toward the only table, next to the stage, he pictured her lying on the bed, in the candle light, and her thighs slowly opened like still photographs of a white rose. The clanging was drowned out by the notes of a silver flute—the waiter led him past the table, past the stage into a dark courtyard, and he saw her in a lighted doorway, and she took his hand, and together, they entered the Garden of Delights.

July 26, 2015

    Such a swelling of emotion rising as I read those words, thinking of the "Gacela" and Lorca's garden in Granada. The painting on this card is so dark—the knight on the rearing black horse, the courtyard of the stone castle, illuminated only from the arched doorway where a figure stands. And now, as I look closely at the figure, it is not a woman, not me, but you, beckoning me through that portal into your world of delights. What a beautiful image to carry in my heart.

    A week later, as I reviewed the card, I saw how prescient it was in foreshadowing what was to happen during that week. I had received the results of the MRI and was told I was to have surgery, as cancer was suspected. As a child, I had been by my grandmother's side throughout her illness and death from uterine cancer, and I knew that it was not an easy path. I pondered my own death, what my options would be after the surgery, and came to the conclusion that if chemo were recommended, I would choose against it. I felt surprisingly calm in light of what I was facing. I believed this card was a promise that I would be with him, which was, after all, my heart's desire. And I even hoped that this surgery could somehow offer me an opportunity to leave this world in a quick and easy way.

And it is Tuesday afternoon, and I am both with you and without you. I sit on the porch and see clouds covering the sun, and I wish them to move so lightly, so you may feel once again the sun's atoms of warmth circulating in your face. When you stand there in front of the class, so with them— so alone—and you point out for them beautiful roads, without numbers on maps, leading to magic lands that can only be reached by impulse, you sometimes see only the fear and trembling that leads to the land of itineraries, plainly marked on all maps from the Government Printing Office. Then you know what magic you are a part of.

And now I am just a Lantana reaching through the screen, reaching for you—and loving you in your blue-eyed Perfection, and thanking the gods and goddesses that let us be alive at the same time.

August 3, 2015

In meditation this morning, I was thinking of your note—how you were with me and without me all at once. And how through imagination and magic, I will learn to be with you, even as I am without you. It is so surprising to find that it is something you have known all along, even when we were together. I thought of the home on the mountain that we had created, where magic was a regular guest, of celebrations of spring and autumn and of you and me dancing for our guests to a yuletide tune with candlelit crowns on our heads. As I did so, flashes of energy began to leap through my body. And at that moment, you were my Merlin, tapping me with your wand and sending shocks of realization through me.

More and more, my thoughts turned to the surgery, which was now less than a month away. Of the family of four cats we had brought from the mountain, two remained with me. Jeremy, eighteen and ailing, needed daily medication and fluids injected three times a week. Boston, twelve, also was temporarily on medication. I knew I would be unable for at least a week after surgery to pick up Jeremy when it was time to treat him, and Boston was skittish when he knew it was time for his meds. I would need someone with expertise to care for both cats. It was a surprise to find that one of the techs who worked for my vet would do this before and after work. I felt fortunate to find her, as many times in the past, I had sought help from a variety of vets—to recommend someone to care for our cats—with no success.

I went ahead setting things in order, carrying out the medical requirements, laying in food, and borrowing a blow-up bed to use in the living room so I could avoid climbing the stairs to the bedroom. I was still thinking about Moorjani's near-death experience and the wonderful vision of that moment that she carries through life. If the surgery was not to be severe enough to aid me in joining Johnny, I faintly hoped that at the least I could have such a vision. In my thoughts, I asked Johnny to be beside me as I was wheeled into the room of glaring bright lights.

As I stood looking out to the lake on a peaceful morning, with the phone to my ear, listening to the interim music as I waited for the vet to pick up, I heard the words of an old Police song, "Every Breath You Take," and I knew at once that it was from Johnny. I hadn't heard that song in a very long time. But he apparently wanted to make his point clear through the words, "Every breath you take ... every move you make ... I'll be watching you."

Three days later, I was waiting in the reception area to get my presurgery x-ray, and the song played again. And the day after that, as I was having my nails done, I heard it a third time! Since that time, I have never heard the song. Only now do I wonder, *How did he carry that off?* Just another bit of magic.

As I read another of Johnny's poems, I remembered the day that he brought home the brown seed pod from the magnolia tree on campus, how unremarkable it had looked. And how days later when he produced it from hiding, the brilliant seeds had burst forth to hang from transparent threads like a hundred tiny ornaments. And he had written about it.

> *And the rounded, silver, sliver of the moon,*
> *Hanging like an earring*
> *From the red-evening-gowned day,*
> *Somehow enchanted him, and now the sliver penetrated his heart.*
> *And he knew himself to be captured*
> *By the forces of silver, white, and red.*
> *Now, he sat on the rug and looked at the magnolia cone.*
> *The red seeds became drops of blood,*
> *Hanging suspended over the white table,*
> *And he believed that if one fell,*
> *It would splatter on the whiteness.*
> *And would red or white roses*
> *Grow out of the table,*
> *And would he be able to see the drops of rounded dew turn red,*
> *And would the red drops attract a silver hummingbird,*
> *Using the straightened sliver of the moon?*
> *And would they be red rose or white, and would each magnolia seed*
> *Flower into another way to love her? J.*

August 17, 2015

What a blessing that magic box has been to me! Every card, every letter contains a message that is so real. Remembering the childlike excitement with which you revealed that magnolia cone to me brings your beautiful spirit alive in my soul and stirs the love in my heart to swell. It also brings a sad longing to have you here—and I know that I am "with you and without you" at the same time.

Surgery is a week away. And I am thinking of the whispers that you send me—the way I can feel you touch my hair, the visits at the most critical times from the blue heron, your messenger (appearing and disappearing, mercurial, like yourself), the melodies I hear that I know are from you. I read a letter you wrote from Spain today.

On the way to Teruel, bare countryside, a shepherd followed by hundreds of goats—the wind whips the shepherd's long, black cape as if the wind wished to dress in mourning.

And in the letter, a wistful note about how much you loved Spain and had wanted to share it with me but how you had come to accept that it was probably not possible. It is not without pain to me, now, to know that it was not entirely circumstance, but I was not capable of accepting that gift. And as I write comes that sense of "always," the eternal present, where I am answering the letter you wrote from Spain thirty years ago. Those issues remain so present to me now. And looking at old pictures today of our home on the mountain—coming back from them is like emerging into the drab moment from a brilliantly colored life. How gray and dull things have become. I am an aging woman alone, with two aging cats—the old caring for the old. How I miss those glory days when we were not so young but beautiful and loved each other passionately and tenderly—our love has grown since, but will we ever experience it again in physical form?

There was something undefinable about the nature of his writings from the box—how he, in times past, had seemed to reach into eternity to pull from it those beautiful poems that express so well the infinite nature of our relationship. And I too, one night as I lay in bed, seemed to reach out to him in the darkness for the palimpsest image that had been so magical to him. An unfinished poem, one I had begun way back in mid-April, that had so magically echoed the lines of his own poem, seemed to fall into place. It was the last one I wrote for a very long time.

Palimpsest

As I sort through shards of memory,
Uncovering lines once tucked away,
I find your echoes,
Unfaded by the years,
Like fresh-dropped petals strewn along the path of time.
Find in those notes, distilled,
The kernel of your love,
Where then and now
Blend into always.

A palimpsest—eternity,
Bleeding through the cracks in time,
Reveals
In that unfading place
Our hearts are never separate
Though here apart.

Ever since the end of July, when I read Johnny's card about Mister Death's chaotic recital in the castle dungeon and had learned that I was to have surgery, I had been preparing for my death. I had pulled my living will from the files, expanded it, and added health care directives. I had given a copy to Sean and Amy and had gone over my wishes with them. I had collected photos for my memorial video and left directions for my cremation. I continued to hope that somehow this surgery would provide me with an easy exit, without the ravages of illness, past the door of death and into the garden of delights, to be once again with my beloved. Or at the very least, bring some otherworldly experience that would give me courage to fight on. I was to be sorely disappointed.

Chapter 7

I came out of surgery on Tuesday, September 1, with no recollections of anything that had transpired, disappointed that my preparations had been in vain and that none of my hopes had been realized. I had thought that this moment was a chance for me to slip away for good, or at the very least glimpse the place where my beloved dwelled. But my memory of the sudden descent into unconsciousness and the dizzying return from it seemed as routine as coffee in the morning. No magic. No mystery.

Yet, even as I lamented this missed opportunity, I knew that I would never have felt right about leaving my cats behind. At least I could be there for them, even though I found it difficult to accept my circumstance. Jeremy and Boston were the last of a family of four cats that had its start twenty-two years before in September 1994. Although Johnny and I had cat companions for our entire marriage, this last family was more closely knit and together over a longer period of time than any other. We had moved from the mountain to the house on the lake with these four. The first, Serendipity, was dropped into my hands when she was one day old, by a neighbor, the day after our beloved Penelope died. Annie came three years later. Both were from a feral group who lived in an arroyo on the mountain, and whereas Sera was sassy and standoffish, Annie slept every night cuddled against my neck.

A year later, we heard howling coming from under the hood of our car. It was Jeremy. I thought he was four months old, but he was a big kitten and actually younger than that. We suspected someone had dropped him on the road along the mountain, a favorite dumping ground for unwanted animals. As was our custom, we had him vet checked and isolated him from the other cats for two weeks. Then the vet had the afterthought that we should check him for worms. A positive diagnosis meant another two weeks in isolation. And finally, as we freed him, in jubilation he ran from the room and began a game of tag with Annie. He had been playing no more than half an hour when he skidded into a doorjamb and tore his ACL. After surgery, he was confined to a cage for three months to ensure that he would do no jumping that would reinjure his leg. We set up a large show cage in our TV room where he could hang out with us. There was little room there for cavorting, so we provided him with a toy that he learned to love—a round disc with a scratching board in the center, a trough around the outside with a ball trapped within. He would bat the ball with first one paw, then the other, to keep it spinning the circuit. Through the months of his confinement, Jeremy remained patient, uncomplaining, hitting the ball over and over again to watch it circle around the disc. And through that spurt of growth, he learned to take life easy and stay calm.

    Six years later, Boston began circling our house daily and calling to the other cats. He was lean, grown, and probably had not seen a full year at the time. He would sit in the atrium and look in the windows or go to the back to pace along the screened porch where the other cats waited to talk back to him. Boston had the most elegant gait I had ever seen. He would stride like a fine horse at the head of a parade, lifting each paw high and tucking it under before placing it firmly on the ground. It was a princely walk. We began to put food out, and at last, with moving day two weeks away, I approached him as he fed at his dish. We simply could not leave him behind. He let me pet him, and once he was captured, we isolated him until moving day. The plan was to introduce him to the other cats when the surroundings were new to all of them. In that way, we hoped there would be no squabbling over who had claim on the territory.

In those first years, Boston was an aggressive boy and would sometimes upset Annie and Jeremy, but Sera would take no guff from him. He always knew who to go to if he wanted a real tussle. Sera was the matriarch of the family, and because she had learned early to use a scratching post, there was never any clawed furniture in our household with this family of cats. She kept them all in line, and they had each followed her example and always used the post. And when Boston challenged her, she always managed to back him down, even as she grew older.

As time passed in our home by the lake, we lost Annie first, at age eleven from asthma. A year later, Sera, at fifteen, was gone. Each passing was a tear in the fabric of our family and left an ache in our hearts. And two years after, I was left alone with only my boy cats. By this time, Jeremy was already easing himself into lying position, stiff from arthritis. A year later, I learned he had kidney disease. Boston was still a bit of a wild one, difficult to catch if I needed to take him to the vet for a check-up, but he had at last come to the place where he would jump on my lap to be petted. I knew they would be my last cats, because I was not willing to adopt a cat that I might have to leave behind.

I came home from surgery on Thursday, relieved that Enya was there twice daily to take care of Jeremy and Boston. She was quick and efficient, but I observed how unhappy Jeremy was to have a stranger treating him, as I watched from the bed in the living room while she lifted him for his medications to the island in the kitchen. He grumbled, protesting his treatment, as he never normally did, and I wanted to be on my feet quickly so that I could take care of him.

I felt guilty, as if I had abandoned my cats. And I felt abandoned as well. Cut off from Johnny. Even though I tried to meditate almost daily, I could not sense, in any way, that he was with me. With the poor health of the cats and my own situation, which was getting worse instead of better as I had expected, I had a hard time keeping up my spirits. A call from Neva prompted me to write to Johnny soon after I was home:

September 5, 2015

    Neva told me she dreamed of you and that you sent a message—that you want me to start living, to have all of these wonderful experiences so we can talk about them when I get there. I had no doubt the message was from you, as sharing our experiences at the end of the day was what we loved to do most. But she also told me something else—to snap out of it, to stop wanting to die.
    Why would you sound so cross when I am having such a difficult time recovering from surgery? I do agree that life is a precious gift—or at least it was when you were here with me. I am doing better in our new relationship, but it can never be as satisfying as the one we had when we were both on earth. Give me time. I will try. I will stop the talk about wanting to die, but I cannot stop thinking it.

    After three weeks, I saw the radiologist to discuss my treatment. I pointed to a swelling in my left ankle and explained that I had been losing sleep because of pain in my left side and leg. He told me there was a place in my side where a lymph gland had been removed that was severely swollen and sent word to the oncologist that he suspected cancer. When I visited the oncologist, he told me if it was cancer, I would have to have chemo. While on a course of antibiotics, I waited for the swelling to go down, as I once again considered chemo and again concluded it was something I would not choose.
    As September drew to a close, I still felt out of touch with Johnny. I felt like a lost soul. In meditation, I continued to search for places where we could meet, to think thoughts that would attract his presence. It seemed to me that happy thoughts were more likely to do this, but my darker thoughts prevailed. A fifth week dragged by.

October 3, 2015

I think I am becoming resigned to being here without you. The important question becomes, How can I stay in contact? How do we keep this relationship flowering until I can at last join you? What must I learn before I am allowed to leave?

Today, I began to recall some of the spectacular full moons we had seen together: along a desolate stretch of Nevada highway where the road rises briefly into the mountains, you stopped the car so that we could watch through the trees the ascent of the full moon—Ms. Moon, you always called her; or the huge orange moon over the dunes at Rocky Point, as five-year-old Sean stomped out a primitive dance of joy, a sparkler whirling in each hand; or you, rowing the boat as our laughter rang into the crisp night on a lake high in the Canadian Rockies with the cold moon shining from even higher in the sky. And then I thought of that moonless night in the mountains near Greer, where we slipped from the car and walked toward the reservoir clasping hands. And suddenly, in silent accord, our hands tightened in each other's grip, and we sensed in unison that there was a ghostly presence in the night. We ran for the car. Once in, locked the doors and drove away, laughing at our sudden fright. Such beautiful memories of being with you.

And at that moment, I felt your electric spark through my shoulders—a welcome sensation. If only for an instant, we at last touched again!

I turned to an old habit in order to lift my spirits. I looked for a book that could offer some help and found, on the shelf, one that I had begun years before and never finished.

October 8, 2015

I like what Eckhart Tolle says in his book *A New Earth* about the plant world being nothing but greenery for millions of years until flowers appeared—how that represented a transformation in the consciousness of plants; how the change from minerals to crystals and precious stones were a transformation of consciousness in the rock kingdom; and how birds represented such a transformation in the reptile kingdom; that all of these, flowers, birds, and crystals, are a bridge between physical form and the formless. And I remember how you loved flowers and birds and beautiful stones! Another manifestation of your deep connection to spirit. Nor do I wish to be cut off from spirit. Yet times like these, when I seem to be, threaten my sense of well-being, and fear takes over. Tolle also speaks of surrender, and I have thought a good deal about that. Is surrendering submitting? Giving up? Saying Uncle? I don't think so, but then what is the right attitude? I feel so deflated, as if all the life has left me—perhaps, it is my enthusiasm for life.

Boston did not seem quite right to me, but I was still not up to lifting cat and carrier to take him to the vet. I had made several trips with him to the vet over the summer, and she could find nothing wrong except a nagging elevation in calcium, which we hoped could be corrected by diet.

At best, October was a difficult time for me, and another anniversary had arrived. Since that one moment of connection, I had felt nothing more from Johnny.

October 13, 2015

Three years, today, you have been gone. The last year and a half has not been as brutal as the first eighteen months because there have been many times when I have felt you near. But I am not nearly satisfied. There is too much of my time that is spent without you. I often feel it will go on like this indefinitely with no real end in sight—with just more miseries like surgery and radiation and sickly cats, more times to suffer through.

But then, reaching for the one place that brings me absolute joy, I seek to find that space of truth and beauty that I can share with you like no other. And the only way I sometimes know how to be with you is through poetry. So I went back to "Dancing with Lorca," that poem I began on the joyous morning I felt you were dancing in heaven, and I began to recite it in my mind. And at some point, your vibration shot through my body—a connection that has become rare. What is this mysterious force? And it is force I feel. And I long for it.

I began to run more errands, to do all the things that I had been putting off. At last, after seven weeks, I made it back to Janet's office. Although she had come to my home once in the interim, I had missed my weekly sessions with her more than anything, as she was my greatest emotional support. I wanted to get Boston in to see the vet but still had concerns about the weight of cat and carrier. And while daily reading my book for inspiration, I was continuing to hope for a closer relationship with Johnny.

October 14, 2015

I believe in your poetry to me you have distilled the love that Keats spoke of in "When I have fears that I may cease to be."

> And when I feel, fair creature of an hour,
> That I shall never look upon thee more,
> Never have relish in the faery power
> Of unreflecting love;--

Through that poem, one of the first you ever read to me, you introduced me to the concept of unreflecting love. Since you have been gone, I have felt the vastness of the love you hold for me. May I love you in that same way, appreciating all the qualities, the special nuances that make you who you are—the total uniqueness that you were on earth—that still is alive in me. May I love you without regret for what is lost, in the fullness of the moment, simply and completely.

And in the midst of my desire for a love that is pure, I considered that there were things about our lives that, had I been more conscious, I would have changed. On occasion, I would speak to him of these times.

October 16, 2015

I especially remember a moment of recognition when you told me that I was looking at you with such anger in my eyes it seemed as if I hated you. And I recognized that you saw in me what I also had seen in you and how hurtful that was. I don't remember how I responded—probably with paralysis, as I so often did. I regret it now. But I wish that my response to the anger that I occasionally saw in your eyes had been compassion for your pain. And when you told me of the anger you saw in my eyes, how I wish I had reached out to hold you close. There are many such moments that I might have spoken, to break through the frozen muteness that I so often experienced, told you of my deepest feelings, of my love for you. I want to rise above this, drop those destructive parts of my ego and my past pain, to live close to the internal presence that is always aware of being a part of you forever.

But in the midst of those musings, there remained the mundane. The next MRI indicated the lymph node was noncancerous, and I managed my first radiation treatment quite well. I had fought for the less invasive method, which I didn't realize had the potential to do much greater damage to my lymphatic system, already compromised. I was grateful that the radiologist had prevented me from making the wrong choice.

October 17, 2015

As I was coming back from the mailbox on my way to the front door, a single bougainvillea blossom rolled into my path and along the walk in front of me. I knew in an instant that it was from you. Thank you for the evidence of your presence in my life. Thank you for that beautiful little flower.

October 18, 2015

What I have learned, through reaching out to you since you left, is that beauty and truth are what give rise to joy and love. I have learned that my desire to connect with you is true and valid, in spite of what others may say or how they disapprove. And perhaps there is a gift in your leaving me—what I have learned in seeking to find you in eternity. That time and eternity exist side by side in life, yet the glimpses of eternity are brief and hard to come by, but powerful. I will continue to look for you in those eternal moments.

I believe we have come a long way together since you left. I know that I have grown in my love for you. I have remembered many places where I had an opportunity to reach out to you and didn't do it. My hope would be that, given another opportunity, I could be a more loving partner.

As October dragged to a close, Boston, after eleven years of being in our home, was jumping to my lap more and more. But he would stay only so long without being petted or combed. He had begun to cough, and I knew I must get him in to see the vet. I had hesitated long enough, and I made an appointment for the first week in November.

Then I learned from a friend who had had breast cancer that the swelling in my ankle was known as lymphedema and realized that all the soreness in my leg, hip, and side over the last months was probably caused from that. I was shocked that neither my oncologist nor radiologist had thought this important enough to mention to me. Annoyed that I had received the diagnosis from a lay person rather than my doctors, I immediately called my oncologist for a referral to therapy.

It had been a full two months since the surgery, and my energy had not returned. I had not taken up doing yoga again or even walking in the mornings. When at last I got Boston to the vet on November 2, she listened to his lungs and ordered an x-ray. I was stunned when she returned to me with the diagnosis that Boston's lungs were full of fluid and he had only a week or two to live. I was not ready to hear that the young one, the one who had always been healthy, was dying. I could not allow myself to believe that anything was that seriously wrong. She wanted me to watch him, to be sure that he was not having trouble breathing. I didn't know at what point I would know that he was having difficulty. Cats are masters at camouflaging discomfort. So I knew that for the next two days, I was going to be counting breaths. The vet would have to wait on results of the blood work to determine whether an internist should examine him further, but I made the appointment to be sure the internist would be available.

I turned to Johnny for guidance and comfort.

November 2, 2015

I got results today on Boston's blood work—all was normal except for high calcium, which points to cancer. The vet recommended to go ahead with seeing the internist tomorrow at 10:30. I remember how you and I agreed, when we had other cats in critical circumstances, how we had to go for it, even if the medical costs were really high. Holding to that standard, I want to give Boston every chance. Although he is lethargic, he does not look like a dying cat, and I always hold out the hope that the vet could be wrong in her prognosis. Neither do I want to put Boston through a lot of discomfort if he is terminal.

I am praying for a miracle. I didn't sleep much. Was up and down stairs all night trying to keep an eye on him. I feel we're all down here in a dark pit, and only you can see the broader perspective. I just want to minimize suffering.

November 4, 2015

I find it hard to focus on spirituality when I am so full of fear. I was terrified and shaking this morning as I got ready to take Boston to the internist. I managed to calm myself just before we left. I didn't want to transmit fear to him. He was with the specialist from 11:45 until 5:00. They did a CT scan and drained the fluid from his lungs. His heart is fine, and they found no mass. So we await the results of lab analysis and cultures.

I am much relieved. Every muscle in my body has been on high alert for a couple of days, and I have been running on automatic. I know we are not out of the woods, but it means we have hope—a little more time and maybe something treatable.

Boston seems much better with the fluid gone. I know you will be there for him if he has to go, but I would love to keep that sweet kitty with me a little longer. I will try to acquiesce to the will of the universe. I love you, my darling. I am trying to make it through this with grace.

November 5, 2015

I was very tense all day. Boston stayed upstairs, turning his head away from any food I offered. He sat motionless, head down, his nose to the floor. I spent much time with Jeremy, who wants to be petted nonstop in the morning. If I don't do what he asks, he literally screams and howls at me. These spells are more frequent now, and I don't know how to interpret them. Is he in pain or just irritable? This afternoon, I finally took Boston to the vet for a nausea shot, and they gave him some fluids as well. I still allow events like this to drain my energy and paralyze me.

For two or three days, we waited. An internist's report came back that showed nothing significant in the fluid, no cancer or massive infection. They wanted to run a test for valley fever, which came back negative. He seemed to feel better but still was not eating well, which is the definitive measure of feeling good. We still awaited a final test to see exactly what kind of fluid Boston had produced. He was spending more and more time on my lap. At least, I felt, he was enjoying being combed and petted.

When the fluid test came back high in triglycerides, indicating he had a lymphatic leakage, I knew hope was fading. I learned there was a surgery for such a condition, but it was highly invasive and had a low survival rate. I struggled over whether to do the surgery, but I knew in my heart it would not be right to put Boston through such a trauma. Another small chance of success was, over several months, to give him a course of natural medicine, which might clear the condition. But during that time, he would have to have fluid drained from his lungs periodically. It had been such a trauma for him I was not willing to do it often, so we would have to see how long fluid build-up took. We started the medicine.

At this same time, I had my first physical therapy appointment for lymphedema, during which I learned that it is a chronic condition and that I could expect to have it the rest of my life. I was told I must wear a compression sock most of the time on that leg, but I was grateful when the therapist told me my condition was mild. The strange synchronicity of both Boston and me having lymphatic conditions did not escape my notice, but the reason behind it, I thought, must remain a secret of the universe.

I told Janet how Boston had been staying with me part of the night on the bed and was in my lap to be combed each morning, how friendly and cooperative he had become over the past few days. She thought he was saying goodbye. I didn't want to believe her.

November 12, 2015

 Boston has seemed to feel good the last two days. I am so grateful for that. I am grateful for so many things: that I am doing better with radiation effects; that I have a lovely place to live—your gift to me; that the cats are eating well, that I have them as companions. I am grateful for my friends who have been so caring to offer their help. And that you are watching over me, are with me, loving me in this very moment.

Boston's condition became rapidly worse. Just two days later, his circumstance had become dire.

November 14, 2015

 It has been nearly twenty-four hours since Boston has eaten or drunk anything. He is spending all his time on the bed upstairs. I have force-fed him minute amounts of food today. He hates it. I have been up and down the stairs too much. My ankle is swollen. Things are so chaotic. I woke up in such fear over Boston that I started to shake. I feared I was going to have a full-blown panic attack and had to talk myself down from this episode.

November 15, 2015

 I cannot rise above this. I have to have Boston put to sleep. Fluid continues to build in his lungs, and I count seconds over and over between breaths to see if he is breathing too fast. He hasn't eaten since the day before yesterday and has stayed upstairs, mostly on the bed, the whole time. So I have to take him in tomorrow. I always thought when Jeremy leaves that I would have time for Boston. I used to give Jeremy so much attention, because he was the sickly one. But Boston, the youngest, is going first now.

Boston, in his heyday, was such a character, so talkative, so rambunctious, with his truly lordly walk. I love him so much, and I feel I failed to appreciate what a magnificent cat he is. Please be with us both tomorrow. I have seen too much grief. I simply don't want to be here anymore.

The appointment was for three in the afternoon, so I had the whole day to sit with Boston, where he chose to be, on the bed. I no longer counted breaths but only petted him, as time and time again he crawled up from the foot of the bed to be with me, rolling over on his back to have his tummy rubbed. He could not stay long; it was too tiring for him, so he would go back to the foot of the bed and rest again.

November 16, 2015

For many years, Boston hardly related to you and me at all. But I see that what he wanted was cat companions; it was them he came for, to be with his own kind. He walked in his own territory, with a certain mastery over the other cats, even though Sera would never let him prevail. He knew she was queen. And that was the necessary order of things. He always challenged and fought hard. He was who he wanted to be. In the end, he realized that there was nothing to fear from us humans, and when he acquiesced, he gave himself, his love, fully to me with no reservations. He truly learned what love is. I gave him the love he wanted, and in those last hours, he gave his last bit of strength to be with me. I believe he is satisfied.

In my quiet moments comes that awareness of such beauty within intense sorrow—the little cat who, within his last hours found a way, after twelve years, to connect with and love another. And how it is that his life is infused with the intensity and the magnitude of those last moments when he learned love, and I learned what beauty his soul contained. And how do I allow myself to accept that moment as complete in itself, to let it rest as perfect, without the need to mourn what is lost, and to accept him and myself as perfect in that moment as well.

When I took Boston in, the sky was dark, and the day was windy and cold. I know, or want to know, that you are at this moment surrounding Boston and me with your love. Yet I feel so desolate and alone. I am so empty that I don't know what more to write—except please send me a sign that Boston is with you.

Later that night, I texted Sean about Boston, and he sent back the message, "I'm sorry, Mom. He is with Dad now with no pain." One of his typical brief messages but so full of meaning for me, the sign I had asked for, because he was not one to talk about spirit or heaven. It was not the first time he had surprised me with his succinct wisdom.

In the days that followed, Jeremy seemed more agitated and would engage in more frequent spells of howling, both at his water dish and when he left his sandbox. He would stare at me as he howled as if he were asking for something, but I could not discern what the problem was. He would twitch his abdomen as if he were in pain, and I began to worry about him. Then he went on another food strike, and again, I searched until I found a food that he really liked.

It always made me happy to see that he was enjoying his food. I began to feel more energy and after three months became eager to get back to my normal routines of yoga and walking. One morning, I took a twenty-minute walk, cleaned out my office, and began to read the journals that I had been neglecting. I could see, as I read, how far down spiritually and physically I had been. My writing was shaky and hard to read, and the thought expression was shaky as well. I had, for the entire three months, continually tried to connect with Johnny but with only small successes.

Now in my frequent telephone conversations with the vet, she was expressing concern that Jeremy might be having heart problems, and it was troubling one day when he became upset by the presence of the housekeepers, an event that he usually took in his stride. I thought it was time he saw the vet.

November 28, 2015

I am heartsick. Jeremy has been at the vet's office or the internist's, along with me, pretty much all day and is spending the night at the emergency hospital out on Country Club. He has "end stage" heart failure, so they are putting him on heart meds and wanted to keep him overnight to stabilize him. I didn't want to leave him and argued—with the vet and with my friend, who was advising me on the phone—for taking him home with me, but they prevailed. Now that I have left him, I know that it was probably the best thing for both of us, as I have no way of knowing if he is stabilized or not. It is hard for me to see through the fog of my emotions. I knew this was coming, and what I must do now is trust that everything is just as it should be. I don't know what these two cats developing fluid in their chests so close together signals, but it no doubt is a synchronous event. Perhaps it says that next it's my turn to leave, that my work here is done. Or it may be clearing time and space for me to do something other than care for cats. Whatever, I know that big changes are coming, which will happen days, weeks, or months from now. I feel so inadequate to handle life at the moment.

I picked up Jeremy at eight sharp the next morning. Although he wouldn't eat on his own, he was resting nicely, and for a small space at least, I could relax as well. I fed him by hand an enriched diet every few hours. The vet had taken him off the supplementary fluids because of the heart condition, and we were hoping he could sustain his kidneys by the water he was able to drink. I was to keep an eye on his breathing—it was to be under forty per minute, and he was sustaining at thirty-five. I was happy to see him drinking frequently from his water fountain.

November 29, 2015

Our family was six when we arrived at this home on the lake, and one by one, you have all left but Jeremy and me. I have known that I would ultimately be the only one left, and I also have known that I must be here to fulfill our commitment to our cats. This is as it should be. But never do I want to live any part of this history again.

It seemed I was always on edge with Jeremy, as one day he would be restless, and the next, lethargic. Whichever it was, I tended to worry. I was kept busy with preparation of food and hand feedings several times a day, giving head massages and counting breaths. I was up early to have his hand feeding ready by six, then to wait three hours to give him medicine on an empty stomach, then to wait another hour to put the rest of his food down and be off to PT. And I found time in between to walk my first mile since surgery.

His check-up with the internist on December 2 went well. The kidney values were up a bit but not as high as expected, and as I brought him home, I was feeling good about his condition. I puzzled over my lack of connection with Johnny over the three months since my surgery, thinking of the wealth of communication I had received from him during the first part of the year—wondering what happened to make it seem to dry up suddenly. The draining of my physical strength seemed to be the obvious answer, but was I ever going to be able to retrieve the connection again?

December 8, 2015

As I was standing in the hall today, I looked up at *The Storm*, a print of the painting by P. A. Cot that has hung in our home for many years. I have always loved the painting as it represents to me the two of us, you and me, our youthful spirits. Because of the way the light was falling, from where I stood, the face of the young man was completely in shadow. And it struck me that even though I don't see you in the physical, you are there, the cloak of your love spread above me, as his cloak billows above them to shelter from the rain. It was almost as if you had sent me a message I needed to hear. It bolstered my faith to have your voice speak to me through a painting that I cherish as a symbol of you and me. It stirred a happy feeling within me that I need so desperately at this time. Maybe my inner senses are reestablishing themselves. I think the surgery gave them quite a jolt.

The very next night, I nodded off while reading in bed, and in that twilight between wake and sleep, I felt him next to me and heard him speak one word, half-English, half-Spanish, but the sense of it left me as I came fully awake. I reached out and touched his pillow, as if to capture some portion of his spirit. Hope seemed to be reestablishing itself in the midst of this dark time.

Then Jeremy moved into severe lethargy and stopped eating. I took him in on December 12, two days before his scheduled appointment. The internist prescribed a severe reduction in Lasix, which I gave later that night. He ate hungrily when we got home, so I breathed easier.

The next morning when I checked first thing on Jeremy's breathing, it was easy to see that his breath rate had elevated dramatically. I immediately increased the dosage of Lasix to where it was when I had taken him in the day before. His breathing eased, but throughout the day, he was totally listless, lying upright with his eyes nearly closed or stretched out on his side, not moving from his place behind the chair in the library. As he tried to stand to nibble his food, his legs wobbled. At last I carried him to his box, as he hadn't visited it all day. I could not bear to see him this way. His quality of life had diminished to hanging on. I didn't want to have to take him to the vet for treatment again. It was such a trauma for him and for me. I thought, through the night, that I might call the vet in the morning to make the final appointment.

I was still wavering in my decision as I got up on that dark winter morning and descended the stairs. Jeremy was a bit better. Did this mean I should hold off? In the breaking dawn, I thought I caught sight of a bird lighting in the tree beside the patio. Hoping that it was the blue heron, I stepped onto the patio and peered upward through the leafy branches but could spot no bird of any kind. And as I turned my eyes to the lake, I caught my breath, for the sky was bursting with color—blue, pale pink, and deep crimson stretching across the cloudy expanse of the morning. A perfect rainbow, grounded in either horizon, arced upward into the sky. And before I could utter a syllable of appreciation, the primeval blue heron, the messenger of my one true love, glided from the top of the lake, across my vision, and quickly disappeared. I knew it was a sign, but its meaning escaped me.

I moved back into the house, not certain of what I should do about Jeremy. At 8:00 a.m., when the vet's office opened, I called and made an appointment for him at 5:30, with the thought in mind that I could cancel it at any time. Even though he was somewhat better than the day before, he would breathe rapidly whenever he sat up and was shaky standing, even for a minute or two. I talked at length to the vet and my advisor friend. At last, I was convinced that it was better to let him go on a good day than wait for greater disaster to strike. I stayed with him on the floor behind the chair throughout the day.

So, with heavy heart, at last I lifted him into his carrier, buckled it into the front seat of the car, and began the journey up Elliot Road.

As I drove, I talked to him soothingly, assuring him of the peace and comfort that awaited him in Johnny's arms. Yet I felt somewhat hypocritical, as how could I be sure?

As they had done with Boston's passing, exactly four weeks before, the lovely women at the animal hospital surrounded Jeremy and me with hugs and soothing words as they accompanied us into a comfortable lounge to wait. They took Jeremy then, from my arms, to another room to administer a tranquilizing shot, and returned him to me before he received the final injection. And then it was over. He lay peaceful and still in my lap.

I left the hospital sobbing, the empty carrier light in my hand, the fuzzy blanket inside still warm from his body heat. Our long journey was over, and I would never have another cat.

December 14, 2015

Oh, how empty and lonely the house seems. Jeremy's absence only intensifies the sorrow of the empty place you left. You are all gone now, and it is so lonely. Cats have been an integral part of our lives as long as we have known each other, and never to have another to grace the hearth is hard to face. And what was the message of this morning's dawn? Was it a welcome for Jeremy, a prelude to a birthday celebration in another world?

And meanwhile, I persist, through these dreary days, as the season's archetype overtakes me, and nature's shroud covers me. I seem to sink underground with Persephone, into the dark kingdom where damp roots reach chilled fingers into the cramped space of winter, where sodden clouds drift in my brain, fogging the mind, and my body is paralyzed by the real memory of a deadly pomegranate. And my Demeter self cannot rescue the lost child who wanders, bereft, through the frigid landscape, seeking solace but unable to connect with the mother's heart of joy.

Chapter 8

I came out of that dark time with the wind at my back and didn't pause to look over my shoulder to see from whence it came. It was only later that I began to wonder about the strange circumstances, the unusual timing of events that occurred in a period of three and a half months. I had had major surgery for uterine cancer, the disease that had taken my grandmother. And my two dear companions, my only comfort in sorrow, had taken their leave. What moved the unseen hand behind this great upheaval in my life? As Johnny would have said in his joking yet ironic way, "What does it all mean, Alfie?"

It was clear to me that I no longer could put off the project I had so long been contemplating, that I at last had been freed to write. I had been hesitant for so long to even begin. There was no longer an ailing cat who needed my constant attention. In fact, there was not even one cat to sit on the printer as I typed, to support me with his loud purr. The house was uncomfortably quiet, empty. It was hard for me to know how to be in a house without cats. The laundry room was so pristine—no cat boxes, no crunching of sand under foot—no food to put down in the kitchen, no medicines to prepare. I was convinced that our two cats had left at almost the same time to clear a path for a change in my life that was the will of heaven. It seemed that everything was conspiring to thrust me toward this writing project. As I had seen my beloved companions slip away, one thing I knew, that I would fully honor the gift of freedom they had given me. I had been committed to their care as long as they lived.

Now, it appeared, I was to make another commitment—to record how my beloved and I had connected beyond time and space. It had seemed that it would be through poetry. I had the poems he had left me in the box, many of them not yet read, and I intended to use them somehow. My hope had been to make a book of poetry, his and mine, but I had written only a few poems before, during the last months, my well had gone dry. It seemed a huge challenge, because I needed many more of mine to balance out the volume of his. I sat down to meditate and ask for guidance.

The familiar melody of Neil Diamond's "Play Me" at once came to mind; the words of the chorus followed soon after, with lovers imagined as opposing lights, the sun and the moon.

> You are the sun, I am the moon
> You are the words, I am the tune
> Play me

I knew by now that when a song appeared in my mind as suddenly as this one had, it was not meant to be ignored. I noted in those words the combining of opposites, the light and the dark, to make one song, one whole. It seemed another indication that this would be a cooperative effort to create our story. I was groping for an understanding of how this would come about. If I knew nothing else, it seemed clear he was with me on this venture, as spiritual advisors in my life had told me he would be.

In spite of my enthusiasm for writing, my body was tired. My focus on the cats' health had caused me to put Christmas aside until I had to finish shopping in one big rush. I was still a long way from complete recovery after surgery. On Christmas Day, that huge hole in the material fabric of the universe, filled once by his corporal presence, ached more intensely than ever. I believed he was with me in spirit—I felt his nudging—but how I longed to talk with him and warm to his touch.

Two days after Christmas. Five in the morning. It was too early, and I was too tired to get up. Lying in bed, drifting. Thinking of that poem Johnny had read to me so long ago, the very first one, "Youth and Art," and how, after so many years, I had found it again. What a stirring it had brought to my heart. What a discovery it had been to realize, in the midst of deep sorrow, that we had not missed the joy of a lifetime together. What a great lesson that had been! And as I continued to drift, three phrases, like the notes of a song, floated into my mind, one after another—Lessons in Poetry—wayward child—sad eyes and lonely heart. Up until this moment, the writing that I was planning to do was a book of poetry—his and mine. I thought perhaps I had been given the name of a poem I was going to write, but this did not sound like the name of a poem. It sounded more like the title of a book.

As I thought about it through the day, I began to feel that the lines were an answer to all my groping toward what I was going to write. It seemed I had been given the theme—lessons in poetry—my lessons, it appeared. When I had reread the poem "Youth and Art" after so many years, I had at last opened to gratitude for the life we lived together, a lesson, surely. Perhaps there were other lessons in the poetry Johnny had left me that I should notice.

A step in faith. A step in fear. The fear rose that I wouldn't be able to make that last step where the first page would come alive, where words of joy, inspiration, and communion would flow through me as easily as words of sadness and fear flowed from me then. *Where is the key? The open sesame that will bring the golden treasury of words to my heart.*

New Year's Day 2016. I had never before visualized an end date on my life as I did today, 1933–2016. I didn't want to be morbid, and I was somewhat afraid of dying—more of the process than the end result. I was thinking that I would very much like to write our love story before I go—leave some note of the beauty and magic that we were and are together. At sunset, I freshened the hummingbird feeder. As I was hanging it, the hummingbird buzzed me, so I stood quietly by the feeder, hoping she would come back. And she did.

She might have been a male, but she sipped the nectar as I drank in the beauty of her tiny body, dark gray—a black head shot through with crimson, a totally crimson spot on her throat. As she flew backward from the feeder and up out of sight, I backed away. A glorious moment!

The last time I had visited the magic box was in mid-August. Although I longed to once again hear from him, something had prevented me, during that dark time, from looking inside. Perhaps it was the fear that my dark mood would contaminate his words, and I would be unable to perceive their meaning. But now I felt it was time. I was ready. I slid the lid from the box and lifted out the top envelope. Inside were two cards, just alike—a painting of a single green stalk with an iris, his favorite flower, sprouting from it. Like opposite sides of the same coin, the two cards carried different messages, one of sorrow, one of joy.

> *And, sometimes, when I think I've lost you, my heart curls up*
> *Like a dried iris,*
> *Like an empty seed pod,*
> *(A seed pod, formed like a question mark, is here taped to the card)*
> *Like a blue bear curled up in his cave.*
> *But your love is the spring for me,*
> *And I love your sharing and wish I could hear you talk about The Bear.*
> *I love you   J.*

It must have been a day when I was teaching William Faulkner's "The Bear." His words brought to mind the tearing I felt inside in times of conflict or anger, when the foundation of our lives seemed to crumble, when emptiness echoed within. After a time of silence, he would come to me with pain in his eyes, or I would go to him and say, "I feel such anguish when we are separate." And the other would answer, "I know, I know." And we would throw our arms around each other and once more be whole.

Then I opened the second card and read the poem.

> *And as I drove away from you this morning,*
> *Words of love tumbled from my tongue*
>   *Like children from a diving board*
>   *In a Phoenix July –*
>
> *And so—healer of wounds that separate,*
>   *Joiner of opposites,*
>   *Sun worshipper,*
>   *Shadow watcher—*
> *I offer you this—*
>   *Moon rose*
>   *And*
>   *Sun rose,*
>   *Joined in you,*
>   *So that I will*
>   *ETERNALLY*
>   *Feel the spell of*
>   *Your beauty.*
>   *J.*

It was as if, in these two cards, I had opened out full a page on the book of our lives, wherein was encapsulated the pain and the joy we experienced in each other's company.

I sat for a long while, puzzling over its meaning. I was captured by its beauty. The joy lovers feel when a quarrel has been mended was clearly expressed in its first lines. Yet I didn't understand what was being offered. I read it again, sensing that this was another message from eternity—a palimpsest. Here again was the combining of the sun-moon image—as in the song "Play Me," the words and the tune joined together. I had been certain the song was a message from him. And now here was that image again. The new meaning I saw in these words—that he was depending on me to heal the separation we were experiencing by blending our thoughts for eternity, not unlike my own words in "DNA":

> But listening,
> I hear whispers of worlds combined.
> Sun-Moon are one,
> Soul strands entwined,

January 6, 2016

In the words "moon rose and sun rose combined in you," you have made me an offer I can't refuse, nor do I wish to. It seems that you have offered me the opportunity to blend our essences into one love story in which we both share equally the pain of separation and the joy of reunion. And in those two like cards that you placed together in one envelope, you have demonstrated how, even as we lived in the same house, we suffered so deeply moments of separation and rejoiced so fully in coming together again to heal the pain. And how you sought then, as I seek now, to make our union eternal so that we never have to feel the pain of parting again. And know how much I want to do this, how honored I feel that you consider me worthy to do this. And how your faith in me gives me the confidence to try, just as your love gave me the confidence to live my life. You are my muse—the one who gives me the song to sing, the will to be.

I had been thinking all along that the poetry was yet to be written. It finally occurred to me that perhaps *Lessons in Poetry* was the story of the journey we had made since we ended life together—that the poetry had already been written in those lovely lines held by the magic box and in some of the verses I had penned the spring before. The idea that the lessons were already in existence, that I didn't have to bring them into being, made me eager to begin to write. The statement that Hilary made that Johnny would help me seemed so much clearer now. The help was already there. It had been there for thirty years.

In those early days of January, I thought about how to begin, what to include, and even whether I should write a poetic invocation for the beginning of this new work, something to mark the moment. On a couple of occasions, I sat to meditate with the specific purpose of composing an invocation to my muse, whom I could see as no other than Johnny. I had received promises throughout this journey that he would be by my side to offer his help. I wrote two verses that satisfied my desire for ceremony and purchased a large pink candle for the occasion. I set two or three sticks of incense burning, lit the candle, and turned on some music before I began the reading of the invocation in solemn tones. I wanted this to be perfect. I was halfway through the invocation when the harmony of the moment was pierced by a deafening, prololonged, and clamorous screeching. I covered my ears in terror, taking long seconds to recognize the sound of the smoke alarm screaming through the house. I didn't have time to recover but had to speed down the stairs looking for a pole long enough to reach the alarm. I hauled it up the stairs, with all the urgency of the Keystone Cops, to punch the alarm button numerous times before the evil intrusion finally was silenced. I sat for fifteen minutes calming myself before I could take up my notes and begin again. That was a prank worthy of Johnny, who would have had a hard time keeping a straight face through my homage to him. I had to admit it.

January 16, 2016

Today was a big one. I think you played a trick on me, or I played a trick on myself by burning too much incense and setting off the smoke alarm. But once I got the danged thing to quiet down, I think I handled it pretty well. It was a very moving ceremony.

Lessons in Poetry

Three years and three months had passed when I finally set about the task that I had wanted for so long to complete. As I read through the journals of those early days when he was freshly gone, I saw there was much that was incomplete. The pain I had felt in my body, the pain I had felt in my heart, seemed as immediate as it had been in the moment of its occurrence. It took me several days to figure out that I was not coming down with the flu, to realize that I was calling up old emotions to relive them in the body as well as in the mind. To recreate those moments in writing was a slow and grievous process.

I began the practice of taking whatever I was going to write about into meditation each day to view it from a calm and peaceful perspective.

Up until this time, I thought that I was clear about the frame of mind that was required to set up vibrational communication with Johnny. I had developed the habit of working to create beautiful thoughts in my meditation to generate those electrical charges from him, thoughts about poetry or art or natural beauty. But the memories in my first months without him that I was reviewing now were negative, painful. Yet that first morning, as I sat down to call up these difficult times, I was surprised when I began to receive one vibration after another to the sad thoughts I was having. I finally asked, Do you mean "yes"? and got a big response to that question, so I had to assume that he was validating my thoughts, but I was confused. I had become so comfortable in my assumptions that I found this sudden shift troubling. These disturbing thoughts remained at the back of my mind for some time.

January 33, 3026

Writing is good for me—it's something that brings me satisfaction. And writing about you brings memories of such wonderful times. You represent the beauty in life. What brings me pleasure now is thoughts of you. Most of the rest is ho-hum.

In those last months we spent together, I saw a sweetness in you, a vulnerability that I had not seen before, the beauty that gave rise to all that poetry. Although it is wonderful to invoke all of those sweet memories, there are others, ones I have been spending time with from the grieving time, that I don't even want to think about. I probably need to take a break, get back in touch with my present communication with you, to find happier places. I love you. You are what completes me.

Once more, I sought connection by going to the box, pulling an envelope from it, and looking inside. I found a sheet of beige linen paper with the antique type of his office typewriter. Enclosed, a red trumpet flower, now dry. As I read, I recalled a memento sent to me by my father, a newspaper clipping from Ripley's Believe It or Not. The clipping was a picture of me as an eighteen-month-old, outlined against the sky, standing, arms flung upward, on one foot in my father's hand, held outstretched above his head.

And he formed pictures of her in his mind, so strong that they solidified, there on his office desk—(sun) flowers lying on pieces of rusted metal, bright mist hanging over the cracked pavement, drops of dew clinging to a section of broken plastic pipe—

And her father still bears traces of her footprints in the palm of his hand, and outlined against the sky, she reaches for the sun;

And now, she stares out from the page of the annual, waiting for the wind to open a wooden gate that leads to one of the secret interior gardens she alone knows about;

And now, it is three in the morning, and his apprehension is born of the union of a spirit that inhabits the house's wiring, and one that lives in the threads of the drapes—and the moon has found a road thru the drapes, and acknowledges her soft beauty, and he reaches across the bed to touch the child so high in the air, the girl waiting anxiously on the page of the annual, and the woman lying next to him, and they are the same, and at that moment, they are all the beauty and peace that he would ever need.

January 31, 2016

Today, I found a wonderful new treasure, a lovely piece that you wrote on the old typewriter in your office. I cried as I read it aloud, again imagining you at that desk, writing out those words, sitting there in the flesh. Why didn't I cover you with appreciative kisses when I read it for the very first time, with praise for the gift you have given me? Oh, my dearest, how I love you, and how I miss your physical form, but I am thankful that you are with me in spirit.

And now, here in this silent house, in every room an image of your form—your photographs, all I have of corporeality: you at retirement in 1992, cradling a loved iris, our cat Penelope at your feet, having planted herself there in every picture that I took that day; or in an earlier time, your face disguised in clown white, a caballero's hat cocked jauntily on your head, in Halloween attire; and there, in your eighties, still running—across the grass—hoisting an orange kite into the air. Each day, I greet your image, and at evening, whisper, "Good night," brushing your face with a fingertip kiss. And in every corner of this home we came to in our later years is a whisper of your sweet spirit.

As our story unfolds, the theme emerges that we occupy parallel universes and touch only in moments. And I think of the movie *Ladyhawke* that we watched together, captivated, not so much by the story as by the central image—lovers caught in the grip of a magic spell, in which he was a wolf by night, and she a hawk by day. So she, as human, cared for the wolf by night, and he, as human, cared for the hawk by day, and they were allowed to see each other whole only in one twilight moment of transition. And they each transformed in the moments that the sun rested on the horizon at sunset and sunrise. It seems so with us, that we touch only for a moment, in feather softness that is barely discernible. But yet you are there.

Just as I had gained a different perspective in those first months, from reviewing the memories of our lifetime once it was past, so it was when I began to write. Reading through the journals of those early days, when I was first without him, caused me to look at things differently. I saw innumerable ways he had tried to reach me in those first months and how I had invalidated them one by one. At last, when I began to take them out and look at them, I was amazed at what I found—how often I had ignored his efforts to communicate. How strong is self-doubt. It had caused me to ignore my own experience, the experience that I wanted to have more than anything. Bit by bit, by reading about it and seeing what a powerful effect it had had on me, I became more a believer.

February 15, 2016

Although I cannot seem to find it in myself to live a truly joyful life, I can at least acknowledge that my internal experience is valid—that you have stayed with me and never left my side and that you are committed to helping me write this book. I believe that you are standing by with, if not the words, at least the concepts. I must, without hesitation, open myself to receive them.

I sat down to reflect on the title of this work, which labels me "a wayward child of sad and lonely heart." I had accepted fully that Johnny had given it to me, even though I had not contemplated deeply its meaning. Had he seen in me the same childlike qualities that Hilary had noted? I had been carrying the vague idea that "wayward" meant "wandering from the beaten path" until, at last, it occurred to me to look it up. I was a bit surprised to find that its primary meaning was "willful, stubborn." I had to acknowledge that I was extremely willful in refusing to give up my quest for meaningful communication with Johnny as spirit. And now, I wondered, should that willfulness be seen as determination and committment or, viewed from its other aspect, as stubborness and intractability? At the other extreme is the tearful, lonely child. It is a strange combination, indeed, of strength and vulnerability. Was this how Johnny saw me now? I was not upset by that, for I knew it was a glance filled with love and compassion. But how did the universe look on my stance? I hoped with kindness, for I could not give up my passion.

Chapter 9

By the end of January, I was walking a mile in the mornings and trying to extend it farther. But I found that each time I pushed a few blocks beyond, I would be exhausted for the rest of the day. I had a number of lymphedema therapy sessions, and it took several months to get this chronic condition under control. It would be mid-May before I was walking two miles and feeling well again.

It was easy to fall into feelings of desolation in those days of writing the early pages as I dove again into the period of fresh grief. I found it nearly as difficult to write about as it had been to live it the first time. I would come away from the keyboard longing for solace, and when the pain became too great, I would again remove the lid from my precious box. As he had surprised me many times in life, he continued to cause me to wonder when his words seemed so exactly suited to my current mood. This day, I found in the box on a ragged tan-colored slip of paper, torn from a notepad, the words to soothe my frayed emotions:

> *Just to acknowledge the times*
> *That*
> *Like a flower in the rain,*
> *You feel like crying,*
> *But smile.*

March 1, 2016

I got your message. And then, this morning, in Janet's anteroom, I heard "That Kiss, That Kiss." Do you remember the August we spent in the White Mountains when that song played on the car stereo, like clockwork, every morning at seven as we drove to the park to play tennis and walk around the lake? My day has been filled with a happy song, beautiful memories, and the assurance that you are always nearby. I need to acknowledge the love and support you have given me since you left. Again, I have been guilty of turning away and whining for more. I look forward, with new enthusiasm, to writing about the spring in which I began to discover our profound connection.

The more I read my journals and reviewed my life of the past three years, the more I saw how I vacillated between two extremes, moving between periods of joyful communication and desolate times of distance. It was not without consternation that I acknowledged I was still doing it. When I began this effort to reach out to him, it was with the belief that I would come to a place where I would feel that he was always walking beside me, my constant companion. But I felt I was not living up to the task I had set for myself.

February 25, 2016

I know that I cannot yet say that I have come through losing you to a better, or a more enlightenened, place; or that I have learned to love myself; or that I am at peace, because I know that you are with me always; or even that I have let go of wanting your presence. None of the above. I think all I am capable of is to notice how it is and how I respond to that.

A few days later, I sought out Hilary to give me some perspective on this issue. She told me, "You live in the magical world. Magic is just a shorthand way to say—the world that's beyond physicality—it's more wondrous, more beautiful, more expansive, more loving. It's the realm of beauty, of imagination, and enchantment. That is your way of being in the world, and you also doubt it. So you have this kind of back and forth between the different worlds. It's your human self that believes that sometimes he's not in touch with you. When you say things like, 'I don't know,' you get whiney because he hasn't talked to you. That's your human self. Your magical self knows he's there all the time. If you were able to be in the magical world continuously, at choice, that would be a different life. It's already there. You don't have to make it so."

We sat in a sunny room, high above the valley floor, as white, filmy curtains floated on the spring breeze. There had always been something about curtains, softly blown, that spoke to Johnny's heart. His presence seemed with us in the room as I watched them rise and fall. As if she had caught a draft of his essence, my companion referred to a scene from a seventies movie, *Black Orpheus*, when the children danced to the rising of the sun. I was struck by her mention of this old film. A chill ran through me—it had been a particular favorite of Johnny's, who, at that moment, was so present in my thoughts. I had watched that scene with him countless times while he had played it over and over on our old VCR. "He's here," I said. "He loved that scene." Later, I shared with her his own recollection of a curtain when he was a child.

The Curtain

The transition from winter to spring on the southern Ohio farm had to be a gradual thing, but I had missed all the rehearsals, and this morning was opening night. The white curtain over my cot, fluttering gently, was the overture, and I sat up on my knees to enjoy the show. In the apple tree, I could see a nest with a sky blue egg, and a robin on a branch. Beyond was a lilac bush, a budding peach tree, overhead, a single white cloud. It was perfection, and I was the only spectator. But, somehow, my being alive at that moment depended on the gentle movement of the curtain, and as it brushed my cheek, it anointed me with the miraculous awareness of my aliveness. In the kitchen, my mother noted my joy and asked me what I was so happy about. I told her I had found a nickel. How could I tell her I had seen a curtain move in the breeze?

A few days later, as I walked in the door, the phone rang. I was wearing a pair of earrings that I had bought just days before. The glittering stone had caught my eye, and I asked the clerk what it was called. She told me "druzy," a kind of quartz that was covered with tiny shining crystals. I picked up the phone to Neva's pleasant voice, and we had talked only a few minutes when she asked, "Do you know what druzy is?" Surprised, I didn't say anything for seconds. It seemed strange to me that she should be asking about the very earrings I had on.

"Why, yes," I replied. "How come you want to know?"

She told me she had dreamed of visiting Johnny the night before. He had asked her to buy me a gift made of druzy. She was used to his helping her pick out gifts for me in dreams, so this did not seem unusual to her. But it astounded me. Here was one of the magical happenings that Hilary had talked about. They arose when I least expected it. After we had done commenting on the amazing synchronicity of this event, she went on to talk about the setting where she had encountered him. She told me he was seated on a lounge in a lush garden. As they talked, he had placed his hand on the space beside him and said, "This seat is reserved for Anita. No one else sits here." I was thrilled that he was saving a place for me and urged her to tell me more about the garden. "There were arches," she said. "And mosaics, like tiles."

I grew more excited by the minute, as it began to sound a lot like the Alhambra, the setting I had envisioned him in for some time now. I didn't mention that to Neva. She added that my Annie cat was there and white fluffy cats as well, perhaps the Persians we had raised many years before.

Later that evening, I collected some pictures from the internet of the tiled edifices in the Alhambra and of the arches in the Generalife, the gardens portion of the castle. I emailed them to Neva, asking if the place where she met Johnny resembled the pictures. She emailed back immediately: "This is it!"

To celebrate this validation of my first vision of Johnny in that Andalucian garden, I went searching for a photo to use as my desk top background and found exactly the right one—the magnificent Alhambra under a full moon.

There were so many times he traveled to Spain that I had to stay behind. He would go to teach a summer session, or for a sabbatical stay, or to collect writings of poets who are widely read by the public in Spain. But as he left, our minds and hearts were always on his return.

> And when I think that you will be waiting for me
> when I get home, at that moment I find the source
> of a beautiful stream—
> And I am in Spain, in a second class compartment,
> a drizzling dawn, a tiny station, a girl with
> an incredibly white rose in her hair, and her
> hair is a garden in the rain where she
> waits for her lover, as you wait for me now.
> And something inside me swells, like bursting
> leaf buds over muddy roads, whose tiny lakes
> reflect tiny moons—it is the night of
> the endless moons, and I make for you a necklace
> of moons that, even so, are not enough to
> tell you what your love means to me...

March 20, 2016

As I waited for you then, you wait for me now, reserving a place beside you in a garden of moons and stars, a garden of cats

Lessons in Poetry

and roses. And though our hearts feel the pain of a lover long absent, I am confident they will once again swell with the joy of loves reunited.

It had been a month since I sat in the room with Hilary as the white curtains were lifted by the breeze, and my mind kept returning to that image, which had so defined the day, to how palpable his presence had been in the room. For nearly a year, since I had written my last poem, I had asked myself, Where is my inspiration? Why can I not write? And now a new question. Why had I not written about this day, which had left such an aura of magic in my mind that it continued to call the moment to memory?

April 4, 2016

When I awoke this morning, just as I was coming into awareness, I thought I was in our bed at our old home, lying next to you, and I opened my eyes to look through the French doors at the mountain. Although to be brought suddenly back from such a blissful moment to the reality of the solitude of this bedroom, the drawn blinds, would normally cause me upset, I carried the joy of the dream moment into the day. I set out on my morning walk feeling your accompanying presence. As I walked, I shared the lovely flowers along the path with you, especially the pomegranate. I remembered how you would point out the intricacies of a blossom—even as I noted the pomegranate's red, leathery, bell-shaped pods with petals sprouting from them—all the stages of the fruit that existed at the same time on that single bush—how once the petals had shriveled and dropped away, the pod itself curled outward into stiff points, posing as a yellow flower, until I discovered its disguise by touching the crusty points masquerading as petals—and how those points shriveled as the pod began to swell, like a pregnant belly, and eventually ripened into the fruit itself.

Arriving home, still feeling the joy of the morning permeated by his presence, I jotted down a poem. I felt his hand in it as I addressed Hilary, my companion in the curtained room.

> In the stillness of the room,
> Where the only movement is the wind's breath
> That coaxes the white curtains
> To rise, billow, and fall,
> Like the wings of a great, enchanted bird—
> We two sit, speaking in quiet tones,
> As your lyrical phrasing
> Calls into being
> The magic world.
>
> As the gossamer curtains
> Rise and fall,
> Rise and fall,
> Brushing the floor to rise again,
> In graceful dance,
> At one with the breeze—
> His spirit whispers into the room,
> To surprise us with the sudden vision
> Of children dancing
> The never-ending story
> Of suns and moons
> Rising and sinking.
>
> And filled with joyous wonder,
> We three clasp hands
> To join the eternal dance,
> With the rhythm of the curtains
> As they rise and fall.

Things seemed to be breaking for me that spring. Coming to acknowledge the many evidences of Johnny's presence in my life—evidences that I had ignored in those earlier days—created a burgeoning of my faith in his unseen presence. The repeated insights I received during meditation assured me that he was guiding me every step of the way. Although I had written all my life, I found a new excitement in it. I would occasionally become stuck in the narrative, but there was not the angst and the tension that I had felt in years before. I was amazed at the rapid progress I had made in those first few months. And I felt that his participation was what had made this work possible, from the title up to that moment. I at last had come to believe that, with the help I was getting, I could complete our story as I had envisioned.

My box continued to yield its treasures.

And he took a flower from the fruit tree,
and one of the petals had, what seemed to
him, the outline of a tree, the
tree on which it had grown, the tree that
had nourished it—

And he knew that somewhere on his body was
her outline, for he had grown and been
nourished by the beauty of her mind and
body.

April 10, 2016

I believe that each of our outlines is printed on the other's soul. We are together entwined, like the two strands of DNA, like the "entangled" particles that affect each other instantly, no matter how far apart they have wandered. The cool prickle that tingles along my skin in meditation is the residue of the powerful surges of energy you send through my body. And those surges forge soulways that are your imprint in me, so that you are always with me, having embedded your soul into mine.

In my writing, I had moved into the events of 2014, the year in which I felt myself beginning to shed some of the the dark energy that had enveloped me for so many months. I had still been subject to deep depressions, but rather than staying in a permanent state of despondency, I had begun to vacillate between the opposite ends of the emotional scale. I was hoping that as I progressed through the narration of the wondrous events of that remarkable year, it would effect a transformation, a healing, of my soul. I wished to carry forward the constant knowing that I was always in touch with my soul mate, as he was with me. Perhaps I could train my soul to stay in the magic world instead of falling out of touch every few days. I believed if the writing of the book would allow me never to doubt the eternal nature of our love, it would achieve its purpose. His poetry continued to support me.

> *And sometimes, I feel like I am with child, and I fear*
> *they might make a situation comedy of me, or,*
> *at least, an article in Scientific American ...*
>
> *For there she is—this tiny, black-haired-iris-eyed-*
> *girl that runs thru the gardens of my mind,*
> *chasing*
> > *butterflies in the mornings,*
> > *fireflies in the afternoon,*
> > *snowflakes in winter ...*
>
> *And I know that someday, not in this life, she will*
> *be born of woman, for that is as it should be ...*
> *And there is no hurry, for she is happy and*
> *not anxious to leave the secret places within me—*

For she is the breeze that moves the waving iris, and the growing moon,

And she, of course, is you.

April 19, 2016

    I took your last two poems to my session with Janet today. I spoke at length about how totally clueless I was when you first offered me these poems—how I didn't understand the depth of their wisdom. She said my obtuseness arose from the fact that they were not written for me then but written for me now, in an eternal space that knows no time. That even though they revealed your wisdom, you may not even have understood them yourself, that the child you carry, who was to be born of woman and who you perceived to be me, was a perception beyond understanding.

April 24, 2016

    Your birthday approaches, everything is in bloom, and I ache with homesickness for you and the kitties. I think so much about joining you there. I think I shall never find true happiness until I am fully reunited with you once more. I am so grateful that I am graced by your energy much of the time, but it is not the same as having you as my companion to be with and to talk to. I am managing. That is better than I was doing for a long time.

    Neva had sent me a Mother's Day gift for the second year in a row, a delicate necklace featuring three, large, opaque, sea-foam-green beads separated by clusters of glass beads of pink and green tints. She had dreamed of visiting Johnny in his garden, flanked by arches, the home of numerous cats. She said whenever she had seen him, he was always alone, except for the cats, and that this time he had asked her to select a gift that was the colors of the sunset. Since she had told me before of her impression that this garden was near the sea, I assumed that the necklace was meant to suggest the sun setting over the sea. She asked me about an experience of yellow butterflies, because he had mentioned being with me during such a time. Try as I might, I could call nothing to mind.

Our conversation was suddenly interrupted by a shrill squeal on the line, signaling problems with the connection, followed by intense static and an eerie, indistinct voice. And then the line went dead. After a couple of minutes of frantic dialing, we reconnected.

Neva asked me in a terse voice, "Did you hear that?"

I told her what I had heard.

She said, "It was Johnny. I heard him through the static saying, 'Don't forget. Be sure and tell her I love her.' He told me when I saw him in the dream to tell you that, and I hadn't done it."

We spoke in hushed tones, awed by what had just happened. Neva was obviously unsettled, even though she seemed to take his appearances in her dreams as a matter of course. She knew that I had planned to see Jamie in a few days and urged me to ask him about it. I promised I would.

Our conversation had given me a lot to think about. The voice over the wires had stunned us both, and I went over and over it in my mind, relishing my excitement at hearing so directly from him. I puzzled, as well, over his remembrance of yellow butterflies, struggling to bring to mind the day in our lives he could have been recalling. Almost the moment I settled into meditation, it was there in a flash. I wondered how I could have forgotten, even for a moment. It was one of the most magnificent, and certainly one of the most perilous, days of our lives together, the day I made reference to in the poem "Echoes."

We were camping in the Chiracauhuas in southern Arizona, having sat around the fire the night before, listening in on a nearby conversation as a woman told of how she had seen the spirit of the legendary Apache chief Cochise. The next morning, we hitched a ride to Massai Point at the top of the mountain so we could enjoy a scenic seven-mile hike down Echo Canyon. Johnny carried a small backpack holding our lunch and a tarp to protect us from a possible summer thunderstorm.

We made our way down the trail through a steep canyon, where rhyolite spires towered above us, and picnicked on a flat rock looking over the desert thousands of feet below. As we moved down the canyon into a valley of oak, we heard thunder rolling through the mountains. It grew louder as we crossed a shallow canyon to follow a path along its edge. Fat raindrops began plopping in the dust of the trail. As the shower's intensity gained momentum, Johnny pulled the tarp from the backpack, and, sitting on a rock, we huddled beneath it, shivering in the chill air that had blown in with the storm. We listened for a long while as the rain splattered on the canvas with increasing force. At last, the downpour began to ease, and we peeked out from under the dripping tarp. We were shaken by what we discovered. A fierce torrent roaring at our feet. In our brief time under the canvas, a flash flood had created a raging river, at least twenty feet wide, tumbling tree trunks, boulders, and all manner of debris along in its wake. We had missed by inches being swept away.

It was as if the whole world had been recreated anew. Freshly made waterfalls shot from the cliffs above and fell hundreds of feet to the valley below. Raindrops, sparkling in the reemerging sun, shimmered on every bush, and thousands of yellow butterflies fluttered from branch to branch, seeming to sip from every trembling drop. With a sense of terror and wonder, we continued on our way. After that magical event, I gave Johnny this poem:

> I found you again (as I have found you before,
> In many moments and in many centuries)
> In the Temple of the Living Rocks
> Where the goddess sculpts not only man-like idols
> But other precious creatures of her queendom.

I found you (as I will always find you)
In her tiny acorn cups,
Lime pine cones,
And irridescent butterflies.

We sampled tart applets
She cultured for a faery Eden,
Chatted with a friendly lizard,
And peeked together over the very edge of the world.

Asked for a sign, she spared no offering
And, with a roar, emptied her magic bag of tricks
In torrents into our canyon.
And blessed us with sudden waterfalls,
Sounding to no human ears but ours,
And myriad dancing globelets
Capturing the sun.

Although I was always delighted to hear from Johnny through Neva, I was also troubled that he came to her in person and never to me. So when I saw Jamie, I intended to ask him about it. But he seemed to pick up on my intention before I even got around to asking.

"Nevara, Nevada, Nevena," he said. "Three Nevs. Is there an N name?"

"Yes," I replied. "Neva. And she wanted me to ask you something." I went on to tell how she frequently dreamed about Johnny and what happened when the line went dead during our recent phone call. I explained that I thought she had been quite disturbed by the incident.

He told me that when he could talk about events like this, which occurred all the time in the research that he was involved in scientifically proving, she would be better able to accept that such experiences were valid. And to my questioning him about why Johnny came to Neva and not to me, he answered simply.

"He does come to you. But he moves with a gentle, even energy. He is not going to hit you over the head with it. It's up to you to pick it up."

So I left the reading as baffled as I had been before, wondering what I needed to do to hear my husband clearly.

I began to pay more attention to the idea that it was my habits of thought that were obstructing Johnny's communications. I saw so clearly, at times, that my waffling back and forth between the poles of "with him" and "without him" was causing me to progress more slowly than if I could always hold that he was with me right here, right now. I needed only to look at my history at all of the times he had come to me and trust that he would come again. Those moments revealed how he was ever present in my life and shattered every doubt.

May 30, 2016

It was two months ago that Neva first told me about dreaming of you in a garden setting with many cats. It was a month after that I found a picture of the Alhambra under a full moon and used it as the desktop background for my computer. And it was only this morning, in meditation, that I recalled to you that it had been two years since I envisioned you in an Alhambra-like setting with a garden where all the cats could roam. The denouement of this chain of events came this evening when I pulled from the box a card with a silk-screened image of a castle rising above a garden beneath a crescent moon.

And here—
In this moon castle,
I wait for you,
Above the gardens of my mind.
And the slivered moon,
When I touch you again,
Will be full,

> *As I reach my hand*
> *To you*
> *Through the hole in the*
> *Garden wall.*
> *I love you.*

The synchronicity of the moment, these visions coming together—the message that you are waiting there for me in the castle, longing to be face-to-face with me once more—all are such validation that it is all real. I am so excited I will not sleep tonight!

I couldn't wait to share the experience with Neva as fully as possible. It would have to be by phone, as she lived in another state. Building drama, I mailed her copies of the photo on my desktop—the Alhambra under the full moon—and the card Johnny had sent, with the castle and the crescent moon. I told her not to open the envelope until I could talk to her. When we did, I tried to create for her, as nearly as possible, what I had experienced.

I told her that for two years I had envisioned Johnny living in a place much like the Alhambra, with vast gardens where cats could roam—even when I wrote the first poem to him, "Alhambra." All along, thinking it was a fantasy, I had been stunned when she described, two months before, the place where she met him in her dreams, a garden of arches and mosaics.

Then I asked her, first, to look at the photo I had sent of the Alhambra under the full moon and then at the copy of the card he had sent, with the drawing of the castle. They were so alike—their turrets and arches. I read her his message and waited. There was only silence. At last she said quietly, "I think we need time to process this. Let's talk another time." I had known I could depend on her to understand how powerfully his words had affected me.

The following Tuesday, waiting in Janet's office, I heard two lines from a song of Billy Joel's that moved me to tears—"This is a time to remember, And it will not last forever." It called to mind special times in our lives but one especially, how intensely we lived when we were in graduate school. We went back after we had been married six years and were keenly aware of what a special time it was in our lives, maybe, we thought, even the best time.

I woke the next morning with the tune playing in my mind and thought how poignant it was now, since all of those beautiful times of our lives had faded, and I had only memories left. But then I thought, *What about right now—the last year and a half when I have seemed to live in a magical sphere, receiving poems from the beyond as we have been merging our souls? Is this not also a time to remember?* Johnny would have encouraged me in these thoughts. His own motto was carpe diem, seize the day.

I tried to ignore my anxiety caused by the diminishing number of cards in the box. As I opened a card picturing a white unicorn beneath a crescent moon, I began to wonder where I would turn for comfort when all of the cards had been read.

> *I looked at the moon*
> *While you were sleeping,*
> *And it became a*
> *Unicorn's horn and*
> *became YOU, and the*
> *Horn pierced my heart,*
> *And purified my heart*
> *With your warmth,*
> *Your trust, your*
> *Love, your perfect*
> *Beauty, your*
> *Acceptance of me.*
> *And my heart divided,*
> *Like a pulsating cell,*
> *And became thousands of hearts.*
> *And my Love went out to*
> *All creatures of the*
> *Universe*

And ALL because
Of you—

I love you. J.

June 12, 2016

What you described in the poem I read today is the expansive love I feel flowing from you now. And what is clear to me is that it was always there in our relationship—I felt it in my own heart beneath the frustrations, the disappointments, and the disagreements we experienced. Beyond those, how I have known you is through all those traits that make up your personality—your playfulness, your brilliance, your wit, your vulnerability. I want to feel that. I feel your all-encompassing love. Who you were in life is what I am missing.

His love, his sensitivity, the unique quality of his speech I could still find in one place only.

And, in Prescott, you showed me the wild asters purple, which had almost become nostalgia—like the periwinkle in the atrium...
And if I am an iris, you are a yellow rose, and when we touch, some of your beauty rubs off on me—and your bright beauty is at the very center of my being, like the golden center of the iris—
I can only hope [others'] memories of you will be as strong as mine, as strong as the purple of the wild aster, well on its way to nostalgia.
I love you,
J.

June 27, 2016

    Your handwriting always moves me, and I wonder if your soul print is in your handwriting. Is that why I feel you so deeply when I see it? You spoke of nostalgia, and when I take a card from the box, there is always such a deep longing for those times when I could touch you.

    Feeling sad, I took your card to the bed, lay down, and placed your handwriting over my heart. Tears trickled from the corners of my eyes, and I began to feel peaceful. This past month, I have not allowed myself the luxury of tears, which doesn't work for me. I can know that you are with me every moment, believe that, and at the same time miss the physical part of our relationship—your hand holding mine or stroking my hair, your lips brushing my forehead. I have to let it be okay to miss that, and I have to know that joy will come again.

    I fear the time when I pull the last card from the magic box and when the last page of the book has been written. I must trust that there will be something beyond that—some new aspect of our relationship to delight in—maybe even reunion!

Chapter 10

As July moved in, bringing along the oppressive monsoon season, I began to struggle with the memoir, and I seemed to be no closer to understanding the meaning of the many vibrations that routinely accompanied my meditations.

July 7, 2017

>Today, I felt the intensity of our connection and how precious it is, accompanied by strong and frequent vibes. I had this deep sense that even though I don't know what the vibes mean, it really isn't necessary that I understand. I simply know that you are present with me in a very powerful way, and I do believe that it is leading to something significant—a bonding, a union of our souls and our poetic sensibilities.
>
>I too often let other people's opinions impinge upon my own feelings, especially about the afterlife. I can be thrown into fear by something I read in a book, such as this thought: the messages that you receive from beyond are not from your loved ones—they are from guiding spirits, different ones at different moments. Why do I give the written word more authority than your words or my own experience? That impressionability has caused me to be frightened so many times. What I can trust is what I know to be true within me, and what I know is that you are there for me.

Lessons in Poetry

For the last three and a half years, because of Jeremy's illness, I stayed close to home, my longest trip an occasional jaunt across the city to a friend's who lived at the opposite corner of the Greater Phoenix area. In July, my friend Betty Marie asked me to drive with her to Window Rock on the Navajo reservation for the weekend to visit a Navajo friend of ours. It was a place I had wanted to see since I had lived in Arizona. I told myself it was time I had a little adventure, but my heart was sad at the thought of going to a new place without my life's companion. On the way there, I found myself strangely quiet, at a loss for words, thinking that all I wished to say was what I was saying in writing.

I was in a strange, almost altered, state during the time I spent in Window Rock. It was a mood that seemed in harmony with the surreal, conical peaks and the etched quality of the reddish sandstone cliffs that surround the Navajo town that holds at its center the legendary rock. Through the red rock's window, the sky formed a brilliant blue backdrop. Everywhere I looked reminded me of trips he and I had taken together—to the Arches, Canyon du Shay, Page, Monument Valley—and I felt such sadness at being without him in this unreal place.

Betty Marie and I trekked from one Native American outdoor market to another, toured a trading company in nearby Gallup, overflowing with finely crafted Native American turquoise, and bumped along a dirt road to visit friends who lived in one of the far-flung residences that nestled in the broad pinion-dotted landscape. I followed after her in a dreamlike state, overwhelmed by the activity around me, having difficulty sequencing my thoughts, wondering if I needed to get out more or if I needed to get out not at all. I didn't feel like the same person who had gone into hiding three and a half years before and wondered at the toll those years had exacted.

The last morning, before starting for home, I followed our Navajo friend up the mountain to gather sage to take home for smudging. Where the sage became thickest, she said a prayer in her native tongue and pointed to a sage at the center that we were to leave untouched. This was a special moment for me. I had always wanted to gather my own sage, and to have a competent guide was important to me.

So Betty Marie and I returned home along the long road that I had traveled many times with him, through Holbrook and Winslow to Flagstaff and Sedona. By late afternoon, we were in Glendale, at Betty Marie's house where I had left my car. After somewhat tensely sharing the driving on the trip, I settled into the familiar feel of my own Solara to begin the hour-long ride home to Gilbert. At sunset, I pulled into my garage, feeling relief flow into my body in being back in my comfort zone.

Yet the trip had stirred within me such yearning and an insecurity that caused me to scrutinize myself with a critical eye. Not surprising, I succumbed to a series of migraine headaches after my return that made me prone to disheartenment.

July 19, 2016

The sadness that had been pressing for release throughout the trip broke out today in a flood of tears. They allowed me to acknowledge how I miss your thoughts, your words, your turns of phrase. If I could only capture those to hold a conversation with you. I miss your presence, the essence of you. Will I ever have that again?

A card from the box had the opening verse from the *Rubaiyat of Omar Khayyam* in golden letters on its face:

> Awake! for Morning in the Bowl of Night
> Has flung the Stone that puts the Stars to Flight:
> And Lo! the Hunter of the East has caught
> The Sultan's Turret in a Noose of Light.[6]

---

[6] Fitzgerald, *The Rubaiyat of Omar Khayyam*, 41.

And his words within:

> *With love*
> *and acknowledgement*
> *of*
> *the joy of*
> *awakening*
> *next*
> *to*
> *you*
>   *J.*

July 20, 2016

And what joy it was to sleep beside you the whole night through, to wake beside you, and to sit at the counter with you at breakfast. There was never a day that was dull or boring or tedious, the way my life often is now. Life was always interesting with you in it, surrounded by the unique home that we created, filled with flowers grown by your hand. I never wanted anything else.

July 22, 2016

In meditation today, an unwanted image arose—that moment during our last weeks together when you said to me in a moment of vulnerability and recognition that it was time to say goodbye—how the time had come for parting and that we must let go. And I acknowledged it was so, while everything within me screamed denial. I knew the terror that was in both our hearts. And as that terrible memory broke forth, my whole body shuddered violently with an electrical charge. I broke into tears and fell into a place that insists I can't go on without you, my grief as deep as it was in the first months of your absence.

Now I am here on earth without you. How unreal it seems. Like it isn't life at all.

July 23, 2016

I have suddenly regressed to a place where I am grieving much of the time. Is it the upset I feel at not understanding the meaning of the vibrations, or the fear that soon I will have no fresh writing of yours to fall back on, or has this migraine sickness put me in such a depressed mood? I need to pick myself up, remember that you are with me in every moment, and stop the whining.

I had been overcome with self-doubt. I knew something within my psyche needed clarifying, but I remained puzzled about what it was. I played guessing games with myself and thrashed about for answers. I read again Hilary's words to me of the year before, just days after I had opened the box for the first time.

"You're still having a review of your life with him, and I would suggest that you consciously attend to finding love and gratitude in all of it, even when you know you should have done it differently, to find a place of gratitude for yourself and for him and for what you've learned from it.This will be an opportunity to bring absolute love to yourself. As you open the box, you will find many of these moments and in every single one of these places, where you judge yourself, you were doing your best. You did what you could with what you knew, with who you were. Our society in every time is at a certain place in its knowledge, in its sophistication. It's all very well that you didn't know. We didn't know. It hadn't come to us. These things we learn together."

July 24, 2016

I have been left here to learn to accept life on its terms. I can't seem to do that. I continue to battle with how things are.

I continue to criticize and dislike myself. Today, I read again Hilary's wisdom of last year and told myself that I am not making any progress in learning to love myself or accept my life as it is.

That first time I saw Hilary, in March 2015, I had no clear idea of what to write, only the strong desire to write something, a kind of memoir that would honor Johnny's life, our love, and our relationship. Beyond that, I had only memories and not even a vague notion of how to begin. And now, a little over a year later, there were many of his writings in my hands that revealed the essence of how wise and loving he was. In spite of this, I had begun to have difficulty with the manuscript, finding it distressing to squeeze even a few words onto the page. I told myself that such conflict was confusion about where to go next in the story. But I had to admit, at last, it was something deeper than that, something unfinished in my relationship with him.

I had struggled my whole life for release from dependence on him to take care of my emotional needs. I had always wished that we be like two trees, standing together yet independent, a goal unachieved and yet unrealized. I probably fought so hard because I knew what a needy child I had been and, I had to acknowledge, still was. And with this admission, I wondered how I could ever come to a place where I could love and parent the child within me. Perhaps what was making it so difficult to write was the fear of getting to the end without the personal transformation that I believed must happen in myself.

At the end of a long week of self-examination, I took all of the frustration I was feeling over my inability to let go of my need into the session with Janet. She talked about the mirroring that occurs as we see our own qualities reflected in our beloved. How the child he saw in me was his own reflected child and how brilliantly he was able to communicate it, revealing how he saw me as a mother, sister, and even a child that he bore—a concept that I remember, in those early days, resisting mightily in my own thoughts.

Once alone, I contemplated how little understanding I had of each message when I had read it years before for the first time. I even felt jarred the second time when I took the card from the box with the plea, "Mommy, don't ever die."

July 27, 2016

Now I am so open to accepting all those images you held of me, so willing to be your mother, your sister, your child, and, above all, your lover. You were so much more aware of the images in the underground stream of the unconscious and so much more willing to consciously participate in them. Was I so afraid of my own shadow self that yearned for you to be everything to my needy child—father, mother, brother, even god—so afraid to acknowledge it that I pushed you away? I am sorry for any time I made you feel rejected because of my own fears, when you offered me such gifts as yourself and your poetry. I cherish your offerings now beyond all measure. I see how I have come to fully embrace your vision and understand the ways in which it applies to me. I want you to know that I accept fully what I see in your words to me, and I love you for your wisdom. There I was, flailing in my search for the Holy Grail, when you already had it fully in your grasp.

I don't know what, exactly, is necessary for me to accept myself. Is it to know that I cannot stand alone, that you complete me? Is it accepting that I am needy, a child, and will never be anything else? There must be a place here where I should become an adult. But how do I do that?

In contemplating my response to his poetry, I saw how my understanding had deepened with every reading: how I had moved from resisting it to becoming enchanted by it; how I had, at last, perceived within it those familial roles we are said to play with each other in all their manifestations, through lifetimes, in many times and many places. The whole tapestry of two souls woven together through time is suggested through his poetry.

His poems I read at first offering in the eighties, given to me as part of the fabric of our lives, weeks, perhaps months, apart. I had thought that my lukewarm attitude toward such gifts was that I didn't understand the expansiveness, the depth of those ideas, that my own density (Janet called it ignorance) was a huge factor. But the resistance I had to being a sister, a mother, and a lover to him at the same time was an even greater one; I didn't want to participate in his fantasy about it because I was too bound by my simplistic conditioning to see to his greater vision and wisdom. It had taken me all of eighty-two years and the depth of the heartache of losing him to reach this understanding and to come to this place.

The second time I read them, as I took them from the box where they had rested undisturbed for so many years, was from a place of loving him even more deeply after over two years of reviewing our lives together. I was so caught up in the beauty of his love for me, the magnificence of his poetry, and the sweet familiarity of his images that I regretted that I had not been more appreciative, more grateful for all he had offered me. And there was the breathtaking magic of the immediacy of his messages, how often they spoke to the very things my heart was dwelling on, that brought me to understand the soul connection that his poems revealed.

And now, as I bring each of these poems to my attention for the third time and write about them, I see the magnificence of his broader vision—his understanding of the eternal nature of our relationship—the dance of those parts we have played with each other and still reflect in each other. With Janet's help, I recognize his wisdom of being able to see and acknowledge the frightened and abandoned child in me, which was also a part of him, and his willingness to be a father to that child. My heart was full as I wrote to him that night.

August 2, 2016

I think of those pictures that I have of you as a little boy, how sad and serious you looked and how gentle. To think of your having such a brutal stepfather makes my heart ache for you. Oh, that I would have understood this more fully when we were together in life and taken you in my arms to comfort you, as your mother failed to do—to have given you the nurturing you needed. I'm sorry I was unwilling to be mother to you, but I hope I was somehow able to be a comforter, at least at times.

Your card I have read many times this week is the one in which you acknowledge the joy of awakening next to me. And this week has been a week of awakening for me to the joy of the total beauty and generosity and grace and wisdom of your precious soul. I look forward to the greater joy of awakening next to you where now you live, awakening to the freedom of being totally open and loving and complete with you.

I felt I had come to a new place. But something continued to trouble me. I had proposed many meanings of the vibrations that were so welcome in my daily meditations but was not completely satisfied with any of them. One day, over tea, I was grumbling to a friend about my confusion and frustration over not understanding their meaning. She said in an authoritative voice, "The electrical charges happen when you are thinking the same thing."

She looked a bit surprised and said in a softer voice, "Where did that come from?"

Then she told me that she had, on two occasions in her life, channeled, once for a close friend of hers and the other time for someone she didn't know, and that Johnny was trying to come through. Then she began in that same firm tone.

"I want you to listen. I want you to get this. The electrical charges happen when you and he are thinking the same thing. It is welding you together. It is soldering you. It is when you are totally together. When you think these are happening in inappropriate situations, it's not that. It's simply that they are happening more, not less. You need to stop doubting your connection with him. Stop trying to control things. Be the free spirit you are. From where he is staying, he doesn't want to call it the other world. When there's connection, it is electrical."

I sat stunned. I could only listen. She went on to tell me that he liked me to wear a special blue—the blue-green aqua of the sea. That was not hard for me to doubt. He had always had a passion for blue. She went on to say that he had an infinity pool, and he thought I liked them too, because they seemed to go off into the stars, where we were together.

"He loves you. He loves you. He has never loved anybody else. Quit looking for signs. Stop looking for birds. You don't have to. He is with you all the time. When you are thinking the same thing."

There was a pause.

"Questions?"

I was tongue-tied. Of the constant questions I had put to him in letters, of the many enigmas I had sought to solve in meditation, I could think of nothing to ask. I could only note the way in which my friend had put his invitation for me to speak. I felt as if I were in his classroom. At last I said that I had all his clothes. The reply was that he didn't want them; he had other clothes.

"He wants his cup out when you are having something to drink because he is there. He didn't want you to give his chair away. He wants you to get it back so you can put them side by side, as they once were."

He was speaking of a recliner. We had two sets of recliners, one in the great room where we sat together to watch TV and another in the library, which we had brought from the house on the mountain. From the set in the great room, I had given mine to a friend and was using his for myself in the great room. One of the library set was out on loan. I tried to explain that it wasn't his chair I had given away.

"Never mind. He forgives you. He is happy because you are connected."

She blinked, looked at me and smiled, "Well, he has given me back."

Just when I was beginning to think that I would never receive another external sign from him, he made his presence known by performing one of the most magical feats of all. Giving me a direct, spoken message. And he had responded to a question that I had puzzled over for months with an answer that could not have satisfied my heart more fully, one that I had posited myself.

August 12, 2016

> Your speaking directly to me has made this a special day. I am much comforted at the evolving connection in our relationship. Even though, in some respects, it is not as fulfilling as the physical one, there are things that were missing then that are satisfying now, so that I can be happy at least some of the time.

Although I determined at once I would do what he asked and put out his cup whenever I drank, I admitted to myself that some would consider me teetering on the edge of lunacy. And when the chair to the library set was returned to me, I would try to fit the pair in the great room to which I had added two more chairs in his absence. In the meantime, I would place one of the new chairs beside mine to take its place. I discovered, as time passed, that he had made this request more for my benefit than his, for the mere presence of the cup and the chair reminded me that he was always with me.

When I took from the box a simple, white four-by-six card that bore those distinctive letters from the university's old typewriter, his playful presence spoke to me in the few lines he had tapped out spontaneously one afternoon when classes were over. I remembered how he typed, without hesitation, without error, as words seemed to flow easily from his fingertips. How lovely that he was thinking of me even then.

Lessons in Poetry

> *Sometimes, when I can be aware of your perfection, the warm-melted-honey of your beauty by-passes my eyes and my nervous system, takes the express elevator, races through the waiting room past the shouting receptionist—no-I-don't-have-an-appointment—and enters my heart.*

As I laid it gently back in the box I thought, *How witty and absolutely lovely at the same time. It simply charms me.*

There were people in Oregon I wanted to see, for I hadn't visited my home state in eight years. Because for half of that time I had hovered near home rebuilding my broken self, I charted this trip with trepidation. What made it more daunting was the fact that once my plane landed in Portland, my path was first by shuttle, then the lite rail across the city to the far side. I packed light, uncertain about my portage capabilities. I felt if Johnny ever needed to watch over me, this would be the time.

I needn't have worried. As I saw that things were going fine, a kind of elation bubbled up in me. I nodded at friendly passersby and, once on the lite rail, watched the city roll by, the places I had known and loved with him when we first met. I stayed at the home of my girlhood friend, Bettie Mitchell, whom I had known since the seventh grade. As kids, we were both new in town; we felt lost and gave each other solace. In later years, we had met Johnny together, in college. Having married, as couples we had visited across the miles over the years, and now both alone, we came together again. She asked me to read for her, and I did with a certain hesitancy.

September 1, 2016

Tonight I read aloud all the poetry, yours and mine, that I had brought to share with Bettie. It was truly an amazing evening because I felt such acceptance and understanding of what I experienced in the exchange of our poetry. And I got a renewal of my awe and amazement at the revelation your spirit and mission has been to me. I hope you realize how much I appreciate your gift and the wisdom you possessed even then, and I can only imagine the wisdom that you now encompass. I will take away from this visit that I am less afraid to speak my truth. I felt challenged, coming here, to share the nature of our relationship, yours and mine, but I am pleased that my dear friend has accepted this offering with arms outstretched.

Chapter 11

I returned home the day before my eighty-third birthday. It was good to be home where his essence was strongest, to be back sitting beside the chair and the cup I had set out for him, where his pictures surrounded me, and to return to the sanctuary of the little library to meditate, where connection was most powerful.

A package from Neva was in the mailbox. She emailed that she would call me on my birthday so that I could open the package while she was present on the phone. Once connected, she explained to me how Johnny had something specific in mind for my birthday that he wanted her to pick out for me. She had said, in that garden of cats and fountains, with the ocean nearby, he had asked for "gems of the sea." What I took from the package was a string of exquisite freshwater pearls, of subtle aqua, a perfect match, I told her, for the blouse I was wearing to dinner that evening. He had bought me unique pieces of jewelry my whole life, and it seemed now that Neva was absolutely the right person to choose for him. She seemed to know his taste, and it was clear to me that the pieces she sent were inspired by him.

Ever seeking to understand Johnny better, I had fallen asleep one night reading Garcia Lorca's *In Search of Duende*, a lecture he had given in 1922 to gain support for folk music rooted in Gypsy tradition. *Duende* is a term that defines that special quality of an artist—a singer, a dancer, a poet—to captivate and communicate with an audience on a level that can only be described as soul.

Duende is an elemental spirit, diabolical, irrational, undefinable, and totally enchanting, ever reminding of death in the background. It must have been the sinister qualities of duende and its association with poetry of the soul that gave rise to the dream I had that night.

In the beginning, Johnny was far away, pursuing a course of study, and I was waiting for him to come home, pacing the floor, wondering when he would arrive. At last he did come home, but he was distracted, obviously not satisfied with being with me, eager to get back where he came from. He was engrossed in the thing he was studying. It had captivated him, enchanted him. When I asked when he would return, he couldn't say. I knew it might be years. Knowing he would leave again and I would have more long years to wait devastated me. I became enraged. I cried and screamed and even threw a dish, which crashed against the wall. And it was at this moment I awoke, my body shuddering convulsively and my heart pounding. I was so disturbed by the dream that I couldn't bring myself to record it for nearly an hour.

I didn't understand this raging anger that had already erupted in several dream episodes since he had been gone. I have never consciously felt anger at him for leaving me. I knew he had to go and gave my permission willingly. I wondered, *Is this some aspect of the selfish child that arises in my dreams, screaming out, "I want my way"?*

October 12, 2016

    I saw Janet today. We talked about my dream and agreed that it represented the fear of many more years alone. Tomorrow, you will have been gone four years. Every time I begin to think I am learning to live without you, I discover that I have only buried my feelings beneath a layer of busyness. Again, I come to the place where I need to tap into that deep well of feeling and acknowledge my true condition, which is that I have not yet reached that desired state of grace—of accepting my circumstance and loving and forgiving myself. I confessed to

Lessons in Poetry

Janet that I had spent so much of my life struggling to be independent, only to come to this place where I don't really want freedom from being a part of you. And I feel also uncomfortable about that. As if it's the wrong way to feel.

Janet talked that day about enneagrams, which are used in analysis of personality types. Mine, she said, was the fear-based one. I told her my greatest fear in life had been losing Johnny. Even though I had lost him, it was still my greatest fear—that in order to do what was needed, I would be required to give him up forever—"And I will not, *will not,* do that."

The next day, in meditation, I recalled the vehemence behind that declaration. I thought perhaps my willfulness might be the very thing that held me back from full communication with my soul mate. Had he given me a clue when he dropped the title into my mind that included "wayward child"? *Perhaps,* I thought, *what is required is that I give up the very corporal way I have been holding him, my persistence in thinking of him as physical. Maybe what is needed is a reframing that I can believe in. He is no longer physical but a spirit. Therefore, that is the way I should think of him, because that is the place where he lives. And I should, as well, be exploring how to reframe my view of our love, which because it is a love between two spirits, not two corporal beings, is much grander and more expansive than the one we had on earth.* And yes! That was the very thing that Jamie had been trying to tell me in the first visit I made to him, two years before, when he gave me the visualization of pushing Johnny off the cloud. I simply would not, could not do that at the time. I even refused to try the exercise. And maybe that unwillingness to even try was what I heard in my statement to Janet. When I went back to my notes to review Jamie's words, I saw that he meant it as a practice that I should do daily and that only when I had "shared the contents of my soul" with Johnny would it be time to push him off the cloud. Only then would I be able to meet him in spirit. In the years that had passed, I had shared my deepest hopes and regrets with him in my letters. Now I felt ready for this spirit relationship. Perhaps now was the moment to set him free.

The last week had been such an intense time—the disturbing dream, the visit to Janet, and the insight I had about it. On the way from seeing her, an inconsequential thought had crossed my mind that later gained great significance. I noticed something in the road ahead that appeared for a moment to be a small animal, its form limp and lifeless. But when my car drew near, I was relieved to see that it was only a misshapen palm frond. I had the brief thought that I had not seen an animal dead in the road for a very long time. I was grateful, for it never failed to upset me.

That evening, I took a letter from the box in which he again seemed to be tuned into my thoughts and experiences of the moment.

> *And there are times when I love you so much that I wish I could, in spirit form, accompany you through your day—precede you down the road, and remove any dead animals and replace them with some of these, so that you would see only reflections of yourself—*

("these" being flowers, now gone, but having left their color on the page)

> *And I would climb into students' ears and into their minds and tell them to communicate to you what joy you have added to their universe, and how lucky they are to share even a moment with you.*

> *And when you were cold, I would wrap you in invisible virgin wool, from pure white sheep that graze at Machu Picchu, and when you were warm I would capture a breeze from the top of Kilimanjaro, and when you were tired I would create a garden with fountains from Damascus for you to lie down in.*

> *And most of all, I would be in your mind and let you know how really beautiful you are, so that when I told you, you would simply reply, like a child, "I know."*
> *Johnny*

I wondered what it was like for him now that he was the spirit he had envisioned himself to be. I had tended to think of his being with me in one place, but now I had the sense that he was all through the house, at once, and many other places as well. Perhaps, I thought, he, as energy, is more like a wave than a particle, and we humans are more like particles that are stuck in one place at a time.

The card bearing this message was one of the few remaining in the box. When I shared with Karen my fear that when I had read all of the cards and letters in the box, the source for Johnny's messages would have dried up, she went into what I perceived to be an altered state and began to speak to me about this. What she said seemed to have an intuitive quality beyond ordinary observation. She told me that she had the feeling that beyond the box was something more, something that would represent a step beyond the understanding that I have now when I am so engaged with his poetry. That once I let go of trying to control things by slowing down the process of finishing with the box, once I let go of this phase, I would find something beyond even more amazing. I listened carefully to what she said, because I believe in these moments she is clairvoyant.

Not long after, as I was meditating, I seemed to rise out of my body and fly with him, become one with his soul. In that moment, a strong current stabbed into my foot and surged upward through my spine to the top of my head. My whole body shuddered with the most powerful charge I have ever felt. Afterward, my body felt limp, paralyzed, as I tried to absorb the effects of that surge. I was close to being frightened by it yet more in awe than anything, catching my mental breath before I could take in its full import. The intensity of the charge spoke to me of the power the union of our two spirits generated, and I wondered if this union was what Karen had spoken to me about earlier that week—a relationship beyond poetry.

With every such experience, I was able to think more of him as spirit, and I knew that I must think of myself in that way too, because it is as spirits that we connect fully. My outlook had improved considerably since I got the channeled message and began putting out the cup by his chair. I hadn't been crying as much, and yet I didn't feel frozen, as I so often had when my tears dried up. I felt content and satisfied with being at home and in a new relationship with him.

And I was coming to care about the frightened child in me and to be more accepting of her. I had such a warm feeling as I began to understand what a gift this memoir was to her, regardless of who else it may reach. When I would think of sitting and reading it over in my last days, what a comforting companion it would be and a reminder of the days when our new love was being forged and deepened. The last four years had been a crucible for the purification of our love.

November 14, 2016

>Just in the midst of such joy, I had another sad dream of you separate from me and woke all out of sorts. As I started my walk, right after rising, I fought back tears, but around the first bend in the path, I found, on the sidewalk, a fresh sprig of bougainvillea blossoms, your signature. As it lay there, it made a perfect bouquet. You still find ways to give me flowers when I am sad.

November 17, 2016

>Sixty-five years ago, we had our first date and danced innumerable times to the song "Tenderly" as it played on the jukebox at Tai Ping Terrace. My memory is that we were on the

dance floor alone. We had eyes only for each other. I loved you then as I love you now.

Over four weeks had already elapsed in November, and I had written nothing since the beginning of the month. When I had come in my narrative to September 1, 2015, the date of my surgery, I seemed to hit a wall. As time passed and I couldn't find an inroad into that difficult time, I sank into a dismal mood.

November 29, 2016

I am coming to understand this writer's block that has had me paralyzed for weeks. Only now, in the midst of the anniversaries of the deaths of Jeremy and Boston, as I feel once again the pangs of their suffering and mine, do I realize that I put my grieving aside last year in order to write. Perhaps I felt I couldn't do both, as I was physically exhausted from the surgery and emotionally depleted from the illness of the cats. As I reviewed once more my notes for the book, I discovered I had left all the details of my illness and the cats' illnesses out them. What was I thinking? How can you wring all emotion from a story and have anything left but dry bones?

At last I felt ready to face the sorrow that I would encounter in the writing of the chapter, to relive once more those awful seconds of counting breaths and the hours of the deathwatch as I waited through a long day to take a beloved cat to his final moment.

I hoped that I was ready to begin the new chapter. But first I was scheduled to attend a seminar for instruction in the Progoff Intensive Journal Method.[7] Over a period of two days, we sampled a variety of ways to approach diving deep into our own psyches to find the source of creative inspiration. One such process was a dialogue with a wisdom

---

[7] Progoff Intensive Journal Workshops are offered by Dialogue House Associates. More information is available at www.intensivejournal.org.

figure, to be done, as were all our exercises, in writing. I had listed a number of possible figures to dialogue with. When I noticed that the only female contained on my list was my grandmother, I wanted to add another. My thoughts drifted back to a time in the seventies.

Wishing to give myself an exotic-sounding name for the role I was to play, I chose one not too different from my own. I literally picked it out of the air—Anahita. Although my plan never materialized, I clung to the name through the years, using it at various times as a password, until passwords became more complicated than seven letters. Much later, around 2006, while sitting at the computer, I became curious to know if the name had any significance, and I Googled it. I was pleased to learn that it was the name of an ancient lion goddess. That information was accompanied by the picture of a statuette that could be purchased online. Being attached to cats nearly my whole life, having lived in a home dubbed the House of Lions, and being, in a most magical way, this goddess's namesake, I could not pass up the opportunity. I ordered the statuette on the spot. When she came, I was enchanted. Wearing a tiara headdress, one breast bared, she clutched two lions close to her, holding each by a front foot. They clung tightly to her sides, all of their claws hooked into her garment.

In the seminar, impulsively, I wrote on my wisdom figures list, "Anahita." The next step was to choose one of the figures to dialogue with, and as I had intended to do all along, I chose my grandmother. I also wrote down several questions to ask her. We were to sit in silence until we were ready to write and then listen for what the wisdom figure had to say. I did as instructed and was jarred when I recognized that the speaker was not my grandmother but Anahita. I wrote what came to me:

> Anahita: You so often think of yourself as a whiner, a wimp, a weakling, who cannot face the vicissitudes fate has confronted you with. But I am your guardian goddess, that feminine warrior that you so rarely identify with. I am your source of strength and of knowing as well as of gentleness and compassion.

Me: What do you offer me?

Anahita: The strength of will, the force to continue, the determination to finish what you started, the power of commitment and the spirit of nature—beauty behind it all. I am the elemental force that powers all of these qualities, the force of life who carried you in and will carry you out, who gives birth and life to you, who inspires you to be a worthy partner of your beloved.

I was stunned by the content and the force with which these words were delivered and by the event behind them—how I had reached into nothingness and found her name, the goddess who would come to me decades later and offer me such profound direction. I had never received such a direct message, and I took it to heart as encouragement from spirit itself to finish what I had set out to do. I learned from further research that Anahita was a Persian goddess brought forward from Indo-Iranian times who is said to have come to Zoroaster in a vision in 777 BC as he was keeping a night vigil beside the Caspian Sea. As synchronicities go, it was no surprise to me, who had been romantically attached to that region much of my life.

Two mornings later, in meditation, the image came to me of a seashore that stretched endlessly in either direction, beside an ocean that reached into infinity. There was a presence on that otherwise deserted beach, but whether it was mine or Johnny's I could not tell. I emerged from this meditation with a poem, whole in my mind.

Pearls

> Strand of years
> Stretching behind me,
> Unknown, unknowing ocean
> Breathing beside me.
> It casts its secrets on the shore
> Amid myriad shells,

Bones of the deep
That echo with the cries
Of tender flesh,
Recoiling from the stinging sands,
Until at last one pearl is drawn.
The harvest.

My life a string of pearls,
Shimmering blue,
Uncovered one by one.
The strand I hold,
Flung from another world,
"Gems of the sea."
Each pearl a moment—
An autumn leaf,
A crescent moon,
A newborn kitten,
A magnolia seed,
A mist-filled canyon,
I count them one by one,
Gems of our lives.

December 6, 2016

As time passes and images of the past grow dimmer, it becomes harder to remember your phrasings, your humor. Yet I have the magic box, which holds them for me. It has given me confidence that you are with me in each moment. I can now accept those inner whisperings that are the voice of intuition and not discount them as I used to at every turn. I could never have survived to do what is needed without your constant love and support.

The pale sea-green freshwater pearls you sent me, the "gems of the sea" you asked Neva to get for my birthday, showed up again in today's poem. I had wondered if it was you walking on the sand in my vision, or was it I. Yet I know it was the blending of our voices in one song in that soul place where we are always together, a paean to the blessings of the life we lived. It is easy to believe that you can come to me just as powerfully and clearly as Anahita did in the dialogue of this weekend. And the pearls you flung from your world to mine, like the pellet of clay in Browning's poem, said, "Remember and be grateful for all the gems in our lives."

Chapter 12

After the workshop, within the madness of pre-Christmas preparations, there was little time to think about writing. Christmas was an easy excuse to put off confronting what I knew would be a difficult task. I was reading a novel at the time, *The Poet Prince* by Kathleen McGowan, which contained concepts about soul mates amazingly parallel to my own discoveries and perceptions. What began as an unquenchable longing for my lost love, and later became an intuitive assurance that he was my soul mate, ended in my recognizing the truth of this author's assertion—that soul mates who suffer many sad partings through time eventually come, through the experience of separation, to understand that they are always together in spirit.

December 12, 2016

The passages I read today spoke so strongly to the lessons that your poetry has taught me—in your story where we as children cannot distinguish our own hearts from the other's, and understanding your phrase "with you and without you" as having no sense of separation because we are one. I remember Janet speaking about how physical separation became a pattern in our life together and that the separation that we are experiencing now is just another one of those. Although it may seem permanent, it is not.

Lessons in Poetry

    I thought of how I must have slept the whole of a life lived with you, who tried to awaken me with your poetic kiss, and of what it is that I am now awakening to—a greater reality of love and beauty and, yes, my own truth. In the well-known tale, the prince awakens the sleeping princess with a kiss of pure love. And you are awakening me into the reality of spirit with the poetry that you left.

In those moments that I spoke to him each night in my letters, there was ever that dichotomy, flesh and spirit, the "with him" and "without him," which was always bittersweet. There was the task of balancing the tension of opposites, a truth he seemed to grasp even as I lived in ignorance. Perhaps that wisdom came to him only in flashes, when inspiration seized him, as it comes to me now. I was grateful to him for sharing it in a way that had sustained me through years of loneliness. Yet it was ever a practice for me to hold the vision that came with each epiphany.

    He never called me his soul mate, but his poetry was filled with a variety of ways that he related to me—as mother, gestating me within himself, or at other times, he as child, floating within my womb—as blind little brother, as confidante and childhood companion. Repeatedly, our relationship arose in his imagination from an earlier source: in childhood, in distant lands, and in ancient times.

    Even in the eighties, there were times I shared in this vision. A poem I had written to Johnny in that magical decade, when our love was in full bloom, seemed to trace our relationship from two flames at the beginning of the universe, through the ages, to the present moment. But I had never before thought of its final verse as the anticipation of union and wholeness that the sacred, soul mate relationship promises.

Love Mantra

In that first forming
Cosmic fire,
I danced with you,
Flame within flame.

In deepest caverns
Of ancient earth,
We darkly tasted form
By shadow light,
Eating for courage.

Bursting into sunlight,
Over thundering waters,
You carried me from Eden,
Captivating me utterly,
Bull god and priestess.

And now,
Poised for flight,
Drowned in your eyes,
Pulse pounding
To the rhythm of your heart
I wait to know you wholly.

Was he as unconscious of the deeper meanings of his love poetry as I was when I wrote "Love Mantra"? Our experience seemed an echo of the Greek masters' perception that the original androgyne, male and female, was separated in the fall and that the love of Eros reunited them, brought them to wholeness, once again.

By now, left in the box, there was only a group of four letters clustered together and a single card. The letters had been sent from

Spain during the summer of 1985 when Johnny had gone there to teach in a summer program and made a stop in the Canary Islands, where friends who lived in Malaga were vacationing. As had happened so often with writings from the box, their subject ran parallel to my life in the moment. When he spoke of the longing he was experiencing in our separation from each other for a few weeks that summer, he was expressing the yearning I felt daily for what had become years.

> *Valle Gran Rey - Islas Canarias*
> *Monday, June 10, (1985) 9 am.*
> *Loving you - Missing you*
>   I
>   L O V E
>   You!
> (Love spelled out in buds and flowers, now dried.)
>
> *Arrived without great incident, things don't change much, here, doesn't seem as exciting to me, I am ready to get started with school in Malaga, so I can get back to you.*
>   *Went for a walk yesterday, I felt you in the ocean's blue mirror and the softness of the breeze - I wrote your name in flowers on the refrigerator, Raul thinks I'm crazy - the three of us are in a small apt., I have been feeling fine, no problems.*
>   *The mail from here is even slower than from Spain, don't know when you will get this, will be so glad to hear from you - if you can call on the 19th. I think of you driving, looking for a house in Oklahoma or Arkansas or in my heart where you live.*
>   *Will take this to Pepe, who is as great a person as I remember and works in the post office - I'll be so glad to see you! Take care, you are with me -*
>   *Please give Sean (then age 16) a hug. I miss him.*

December 15, 2016

    Your message of love written in faded, now dried, flowers is so fragile yet still perfect, and not wanting to disturb it further, I took a picture of the letter, folded the page carefully, and slid it gently back into the envelope in order not to destroy the delicate message. I remembered the many times you had written my name in flowers to welcome me home. And will you write my name in stars to welcome me once again?

    The flower he enclosed in the next letter had not lost its color. It was a tiny, delicate orange, five-petaled blossom.

Please give Sean   *Valle Gran Rey*
A hug   *La Gomera*
                             Islas
                             Canarias

                           Thursday, June 13
Dearest Anita,
    I am well, no problems, tomorrow we take the ferry to Tenerife,
    So we can get a plane on Saturday morning for Malaga. Will mail this there,
It may be faster. (The letter was postmarked June 17.)
Last evening we had dinner (filet of tuna for me, again) at a small restaurant looking across the hibiscus to the sun slipping into the ocean, and I missed you so much—
The movement of the hibiscus leaves in the breeze,
The sudden flight of swallows across the sun,
The reflection of the wine on the table,
    All became,
    Missing you,
Until I felt for a few moments

I "was" nothing more than missing you.
Anxious to get started with the classes, so I can get back to you, my love.
Raoul and Shirley just returned from a walk
With two gifts--
A bunch of tiny bananas, like toys,
And a papaya the size of a small watermelon.
There is a fiesta (minor) this evening with a procession featuring drums and castanets (so says the announcement.) and I love you and don't know how you got to be so beautiful, so say I, Who will love you forever.
Will write more about here when we get to Malaga. J.

December 12, 2016

How did you get to be so absolutely charming with these words,"say I." How those words moved me, how they brought back to me the essence of your personality, the part of you I miss the most. I do not miss your love, because I feel it with me so much of the time, but I can rarely grasp that unique self—that individual expression that was yours alone. It is that I wept for early this morning on waking, and through the day, and even now.

June 29 (1985)
Dearest Anita:
On the bus from Malaga to Sevilla—olive trees to the horizon—on the seat a map of Spain, and Lorca's poetry.
Map of roads
Map of hearts—
The fields of olive trees open and close like a fan - (Lorca)

> Now, great fields of sunflowers - Griasoles -all turned to the sun, to the east, now an empty hill. I think of you on the hill
>
> > Facing the sunflowers—
> > I am a sunflower
> > You are our love
> > > Our sun
> > > Our light
> > > We love you

And on the other side of the page—

> > > June 30
> > > Sevilla
> Hot, sitting in lobby, writing to my true love, have seen 400 year-old magnolia trees, I send you a green leaf that will be brown
> > When it arrives,
> > But full of love
> > For you from
>
> > J.
>
> I am well, tomorrow to Madrid, gateway to home, to you, my dearest sweet love!
> Tell Sean
> I think of him every day.

> > > July 6,
> > > > noon
> > > Saturday
>
> Dearest Anita:
> The group has gone off to Toledo—felt like taking it easy today-write to you, wash my jeans, go to post office.

I am fine- have been helping students quite a bit-picked up a train schedule booklet, help them make reservations for after classes, help with the Metro, etc. Had a good trip to Segovia on the 4th of July, picnic on way back with hot dogs and wine. Played volleyball---few sore muscles around ribs.

Called Celaya last night but he is leaving today for the north, until September—am sorry I won't get to see him, he was very nice, he is pretty famous now, the TV people were to be there last night covering his departure. Mainly sorry I won't be able to introduce Celaya to John—I still haven't been able to contact young poet (Cuenca) will call later today.

I have taken care of my reservations—and that worked out great! The 25th is a national holiday and so all the classes are giving finals on Wed., 24th. It has been a good experience, but I miss you so much, and I love you more every day—
Take care, see you soon—
I love
YOU!

(The Y, a stem in the shape of a Y with a flower on one branch, a leaf on the other.)
Jo

December 30, 2016.

I think of Rumi, dear Love,

> Listen to the story told by the reed,
> of being separated.

> "Since I was cut from the reedbed,
> I have made this crying sound.

> Anyone apart from someone he loves
> Understands what I say.
>
> Anyone pulled from a source
> Longs to go back."[8]

Although I thought, at the beginning of December, that I was ready to write the next chapter, by the end of the month I realized I was not. There was something about that time, emerging from surgery, that I still did not understand. One of the exercises alluded to in the Progoff workshop was a Dialogue with Work. I sat down to try my hand at it.

December 31, 2016

Me: What was the heart of that dark time?

Lessons in Poetry: It was a death as depicted in the card from Johnny and a resurrection brought about by your determination to carry out your commitment. So it was true that you were between worlds for much of that time, drawing strength from that source to see the cats through their transition without crashing—by offering them love and comfort and being with them through their illnesses. You provided an atmosphere of love, and you need to see how strong and brave you were in order to do justice to this. Maybe you were right to leave out the whining parts.

I understood that it was a psychological death and resurrection of which the Work spoke, but I needed more. Finally, I went back to learn what it was.

---

[8] Barks, *The Essential Rumi*, 17–18.

January 11, 2017

Me: When I began you, I felt hopeful, thought I could produce something Romantic, soulful, that would create an atmosphere of magic, of longing, and expose my deepest love for my Prince of Poetry. A work that would move anyone who read it, show them what an unusual and magnificent person my true love is. Create something poetic. In the beginning, it seemed this was possible. But somehow, with chapter 7, that has been lost. It was a time without him, when I couldn't connect, and anything I try to write seems simplistic and mundane. But it was a time of deep difficulty for me, and I can't seem to capture that, how hard it was to try to do my cats justice, to give them the care that they deserved. How I feared that I was not living up to my commitment to them, because I felt so bad myself. Why do I shrink so mightily from this task. Can you advise me? What do you want of me? For your benefit—to make you as beautiful as I can—where should I go with this chapter 7 that has been such a difficult one for me?

Lessons in Poetry: Start with telling the truth about how you feel—done in, deserted, abandoned—and how as you fear being abandoned, you fear abandoning Jeremy and Boston. Yet it is almost a task too great. It is almost beyond your physical capability, for even as they need you to be there on the floor, you can no longer kneel. Even as they need your healing hands, you have no energy to give. How do you heal yourself and heal them, as well? It was an impossible task, and the sorrow of knowing you could not give enough only added to your despondency. There was no one else to rely on. There was nothing to do but watch each of them dying, struggling for breath as you counted, second by second, minute by minute, hour upon hour, as each one struggled through the last days of his life. This was the very bottom of the deep valley, the end of abandonment.

And then, to put each in a carrier, and start the long, last trip to the vet, telling him that it would be all right, that soon he could breathe free and be with Johnny. At the same time you felt you were lying, that you were betraying them, when you knew you would come home without each of them, with an empty carrier, a blanket even now losing the warmth of a soft body.

And how, in that same driveway, three years before, you had urged your beloved into the car, telling him it would be okay, not knowing that you would never bring him home, and he, feeling betrayed, and you, the unknowing betrayer.

I had one last dialogue to write before I could begin the chapter—a dialogue with Boston. He had ever been a bit of an outsider, which I felt sad about. I needed to understand his place in our family. Once that had been accomplished, I was at last ready to write chapter 7.

One morning, months later, I opened my blinds to see the California pepper tree, which has shaded our patio for many years, broken in half and the whole top of it resting on the water. I thought of an old friend, how everything to her was part of a great synchronicity—every scorpion in her house or dead bird in her yard was a symbol, calling attention to something in her life. I thanked her silently for that insight as I wondered if this tree symbolized anything for me—a breaking? Or, remembering this morning, as I threw back the covers and sat up in bed, I had thought of the line in Leonard Cohen's "Anthem":

There is a crack in everything,
That's how the light gets in.

Remembering that, I thought, *Does this mean that my darkened life has been taken away and the light of the sun will come streaming in?*
As I sat down to meditate, I suddenly understood that writing this memoir has been a journey of the soul, not toward total

transformation as I had always hoped, but of finally recognizing my soul mate—and of an awareness of moving toward a perfect union with him. I never called him my soul mate when he was here. I never realized how much alike we were until others began to point it out. I know in my heart that somewhere, in the vast universe, this perfect union already exists—all I need do is experience it, as I have already, so often, in brief moments. And I realized it was time to end the book.

But, even further, what I recognized is that I have come to know myself so well—that underneath all of my striving to be a thoroughly liberated woman through my life, I am an old-style Romantic at heart, a relic of the times, ill at ease in the mechanical twenty-first century, a century of the brain, not of the heart. That is the part of me his soul always acknowledged and spoke to. A friend wrote a poem to me once, suggesting I give up my search for independence and embrace my one true love.

So maybe the tree was a symbol. In its breaking, the core of it—its very heart—was exposed to the light.

For so long, I have feared drawing the last card from the magic box, yet at last the moment has come—February 16, 2017. As I hold the card, I caress it and marvel at the wonders that have been revealed to me in the two years since I rediscovered its contents, in the cabinet at the back of the closet. Once again, it seems there is meaning in it, especially relevant to this time and this place. The card is plain white, so plain that I don't even notice at first the eagle in flight embossed upon it and a feather, also embossed, beside it. And inside his words:

White on White—
White feathers of white birds,
White shadows of white roses,
Moonlight Memories
Of
Moments with You.
Love,
J.

And beneath the signature is taped a delicate white feather. The bird, a symbol of flying free. The feather, a symbol of spirit. To me a promise of something higher and more ethereal to come, beyond the words contained in this box. My fear is calmed. My hope soars.

And I recognize how what I once only dreamed has become real for me through the lessons in the poetry he left me. And how his insights and mine have combined to allow me to see the eternal quality of our love and the very real connection between flesh and spirit that our love has allowed, a love that has its deepest expression through poetry.

From the first days of our meeting, it was so. Whenever he shared a poem with me, he would linger over the parts of it that spoke to him, marveling at Keats's "joy of unreflecting love" and dwelling on the pairing of beauty and truth. It was his affection for such lines in Browning's "Youth and Art" that teased my memory after he was gone, so that finally I searched until I found them:

Why did not you pinch a flower
In a pellet of clay and fling it?

When those lines, seeds he had planted long ago, carrying remorse at a failure to connect, did return to me nine months after he was gone, they came with an impact and an understanding that I could not have grasped in those far-off days. I rejoiced that the choice we made then had led to a lifetime of experience together. The recognition brought with it the first momentary glimmer of light in the palpable darkness, an admission that life with him had been worth the anguish I was suffering.

And that June morning on the patio, as I was only beginning to shake off some of the darkness, my vision of him in that timeless place translated into the lines of "Dancing with Lorca." When I connected with my muse in that moment, I became conscious of a source of wisdom I had not known before.

In every step along the way, new insight, new experience was propelled or illuminated by poetry in some way. In meditation,

Lessons in Poetry

visualizing our hearts connected by light, I was reciting lines of poetry when that first charge of his electrical energy surged through my body. It is this one aspect of my experience of finding connection with Johnny outside of time, these at first strange but now familiar vibratory impulses that continued to puzzle me. I was always searching for the meaning behind them. I had the sense, early on, that when my mind stumbled into places that resonated with both of us, this energetic communication was established. I had written to him in my nightly letter that I believed his presence in vibration was leading to a bonding, a union of our souls and poetic sensibilities. Yet my rational mind would not allow the validity of those conclusions. I had constantly supplied good reasons to discount such notions.

This vacillation between faith and the demon of disbelief has been with me throughout this process. Intuition is a quiet and a fragile thing, and there were voices in my mind that shouted much louder for attention. The skeptic would not give up her position, perhaps rightly so. Assumptions are meant to be challenged. Yet the angst in the questioning was painful.

My mind at last came to rest at this place. As Johnny had written in the first piece I found, pressed within the flyleaf of the book *Andalucia y Garcia Lorca,* "Sensation is connection," it is through the sensation of vibration I experience the harmony of connection, which is untranslatable and defies explanation. I found my conclusions validated in a statement by Michael Newton in *Destiny of Souls,* where he states that he has concluded from thousands of interviews that the phenomenon called "harmonic resonance" is a vehicle for the language of the spirit and an avenue to "soul unification." And I thought, *Ah, Johnny speaks to me now in the language of the soul.*

After I lost my beloved, as the shattered pieces of my mind began to coalesce, they formed around a single thought—*I must learn somehow to connect again with him.* It was that intention that drove me, single-mindedly, toward a goal. Had I inhabited a more peaceful body, a less skeptical mind, I might have perceived more easily that, like the shining sliver of the crescent tucked within the shadow of the full moon, I was already there. But I have required many lessons and expect many more to move toward a place of total peace, acceptance, and love. And what better way to learn than through poetry, for it is, after all, the language of love.

In my time of greatest need, I found, in a shoebox, the garden of poetry he left for me that I will ever hold in my heart. That garden is more magical and more lasting than even my childhood garden that grew in the shadow of Rumpty Dudget's tower and ultimately faded away. Johnny loved flowers, to grow them and to give them, and his flower offerings were a constant throughout my life. He would come into the house, from tending the yard, and offer me a sprig of white or pink oleander from the hedge, a twig of the brilliant bougainvillea that climbed the terrace wall, a rose from the bed out front. Always, there were the leaves and blossoms pressed within his cards and letters. I will ever remember the day that I stepped off the plane and rushed from the gate, eager to see him, and spied, a few feet ahead, a hand extended from behind a pillar, holding a single rose. And I knew it could be no other.

Poetry, the language of love, has spoken to my heart through the most intense period of my life. But what of the language of the soul? Perhaps the language of the soul has no words, only thoughts, thoughts of harmony and resonance, of beauty and truth. A language that I don't yet understand and perhaps never will, not until he beckons to me in a dream from the threshold of the world beyond. Or when, from below his moon castle, he reaches through the hole in the garden wall, clasps my hand, and pulls me into his kingdom.

Epilogue

Through poetry, Johnny shared some of the deepest contents of his soul with me, which have been recorded herein. There was also a very private side of him. In his later years, he seemed to turn inward to examine the forces in his life that shaped him: those formative childhood experiences as well as the study of Spanish poetry that he had dedicated his life to. He turned these recollections into several vignettes. Some of these stories, he shared with me. I include these and others here to more fully complete his portrait. I don't recall his sharing this list of beliefs, which I found among the stories I knew and the ones I did not. I surely would not have forgotten the reference to me, his Virgo companion.

BELIEFS

1. Relativity
2. Perhaps patriarchy has had its chance. Matriarchy deserves a try.
3. Euripides had a great idea. The next time men prepare for war, have women cut them off.
4. When I die, I don't know what will happen. Maybe nothing, maybe something, but whatever it is, I believe that whatever happens to me, happens to everyone.
5. Fear and threats do not produce spirituality.
6. Diversity is the greatest single asset of America.
7. Virgos can be lovable.

Hilary had noted to me at one time that the metaphor that had resonated most profoundly with my spirit, the tale of *Rumpty Dudget's Tower*, had been drawn from the secular world, whereas, most often, metaphors that are central in spiritual life are taken from religion. This secular element in our spirituality was another aspect that united Johnny and me. We both grew up steeped in a religion that failed to reach us—his Presbyterian, mine Pentecostal. We continued into adulthood, feeling a childhood enchantment with the magical world. His is revealed most fully in the vignette "Look Out, Jesus, the Winged Monkeys Will Get You."

I feel closest to him when I read his writings.

Look Out, Jesus, the Winged Monkeys Will Get You

On approaching the Trenton, Ohio, (population 100), First Presbyterian Church, the visitor has a choice; it's either take the stairs leading up to the main room, where Sunday services are held, or take the stairway leading down to the basement, where Sunday school is held. It doesn't seem like a significant choice, but for me, a third-grader from a farm a few miles away, it is like choosing between Heaven and Hell.

Furthermore, the customary archetypal patterns represented by "up" and "down," are reversed, or so it seemed. I usually feel "up" in the basement, and I am often "down" when I am upstairs. There are several factors involved in the basement experience. There are several pictures of a smiling Jesus on the walls—looking down from Heaven, or reaching out to a group of children. The Sunday school teacher is a young girl, who speaks excitedly about meeting Jesus in Heaven. And she has other gifts to offer. She has a copy of *The Wizard of Oz*, as well as several of the other books that followed the successful original by L. Frank Baum. And she lends them to me, one at a time. When I finish one volume, I return it to her before Sunday school, and the next Sunday, she will have a new volume for me. And so, down in the basement, there are smiles, Jesus, frequent references to Heaven, and, by association, the magical world of Oz. And that is Part One of my Sundays; unfortunately, there is a Part Two.

So, I say goodbye to my teacher and trudge (children should not have to trudge) dutifully up the stairs for the Sunday service. The first thing I notice is that it must be twenty degrees warmer up here, on this July morning. Hot as hell. But I couldn't say that word, although the minister certainly used it often. Everyone seems to have a fan, courtesy of the Trenton Barber Shop—"When you need to look your best."—The music is marginal, at best. There is no official chorus, just one small organ and the entire congregation. It's always the first and last stanzas, and the singing is often more like moaning to a slow beat, slightly off key. There is one song that seems to spark some enthusiasm, with a faster beat, called "Onward Christian Soldiers." In the basement, everything seems to be smiles and love, but now it's turned rather ferocious, as we go "marching as to war, with the cross of Jesus, going on before." Years later, I will wonder if "Christian soldiers" is an oxymoron. And I never quite understood the function of the cross in this song. I had seen a movie about the Middle Ages, in which an army beat down the doors to a castle. "Is the cross being used like a battering ram?" I ask my mother. "Of course not," she replies, with a disgusted look.

One of the scariest mornings upstairs involved the minister's statement that "thinking something is just as bad as doing it, and will get you to Hell just as fast." As soon as I heard this, I was sure it was all over. I doubled up, with my head between my legs, and my mother leaned over and asked, "Are you sick?" "I'm dead," I replied. My friend, Jimmy, had already showed me how this works. "Try not to think of an elephant," he advised me.

If the term "show and tell" had been invented, I might have understood better the nature of the minister's sermons. Lots of "tell," very little "show," with many references to an angry God, and with

Hell as our most likely destination. And always the appropriate Biblical reference for verification. Sometimes he would trick me. I remember a specific morning in July, when he began: "As I drove in this morning, this glorious, summer morning, I observed the golden wheat fields, shimmering under a deep blue sky." "Wait a minute," I said to myself, moving to a sitting up position from my customary slouch, "he is showing us something." And it was something I could appreciate, for I had often climbed to the top of a small hill to observe the wheat fields, especially when the wind was into finger painting in the fields. But without taking a breath, he continued, "Yes, I observed the wheat fields, and I was reminded of Jeremiah 12:13---They have sown wheat, but shall reap thorns ... and they shall be ashamed of your revenues because of the fierce anger of the Lord." And I say, verily, that I had been had. And not just once. Up there, with anger and threats and an eye for an eye, a tooth for a tooth, and judgments, up there in Hell—forced to leave the basement, down there, in Heaven, with forgiveness and turn the other cheek.

It is true that, sometimes, I experienced some confusion regarding Jesus and the world of Oz, interchanging Jesus and his Disciples on the road to Galilee and Dorothy and her needy crew on the road to the Emerald City. And occasionally, it was Jesus, behind the curtains, operating the switches and buttons in the Emerald City. Sometimes, in my frequent dreams of Hell, with the earth opening up, flames reaching skyward, Jesus would come to my rescue, and hold out his hand to me, like in the picture on the wall, downstairs in Heaven. Once, it got very confusing, for above Jesus I could see those scary primates of the Wicked Witch, and I shouted, "Look out, Jesus, the winged monkeys will get you."

I am old now, but still relatively optimistic. I just want to thank the beautiful, young girl, who in my mind has never aged, thank her for her smile, and her introduction into my life of some truly magic moments---not over the rainbow—but in the basement of the First Presbyterian Church of Trenton, Ohio, (population 100).

Gifts

Geronimo!

Sometimes a gift may not be recognized as a gift. It is a November morning, ruled by the wind, trying to snow, no school today. I am alone with my nine years, and Mr. Boredom strolls in. My mother's closet yields shoe boxes filled with old photographs—good for five minutes—lots of shoes, and in the corner, half-hidden by a raincoat, a black umbrella. I grasp the wooden handle, make a couple of sword thrusts, but with only one of the Three Musketeers present, my interest wanes. Then a plane, left over from a recent movie, soars across my mind. A small chair gives me access to the top of a tall chest of drawers, next to a bed, covered with a spread, featuring robins and blue birds. All signs point to a new chapter in the history of flight; I click the umbrella into the open position. All systems are go. Geronimo! But in midflight, I become aware of some kind of movement near the doorway. My crash landing among the birds on the spread, and my mother's words are simultaneous. "Are you ready to accept the responsibility for someone's death? You know that you must never open an umbrella in the house." And, suddenly, me, my mother and the hair brush were alone. For many years, I referred to this incident in discussions involving parental abuse. "How would you like to be punished for such a stupid belief?" I would ask.

Later in life, I became interested in trying to understand a rather strong spiritual belief system that I possessed. What were its origins? Certainly not upstairs in the Trenton Presbyterian Church, that tended to produce, alternately, boredom and fear. And my perception of the umbrella incident began, slowly, to change. I could not say that my mother was a religious person, in the traditional sense, but she had a strong belief that not everything in the universe can be explained through a process of physical reasoning. For most of my life, whenever I ate something that I liked (Rice Krispies, for example), a bright, red rash would appear on my left cheek, by my ear. Some people claimed to see the shape of a bird in the rash. My mother claimed that as I was coming into the world, a bird flew into the window of the second-floor bedroom, and that was the origin of the rash.

I thank her for the gift.

The Agate

Twenty-fourth and Broadway, in South Phoenix, is not a place you would normally consider as a good place to look for a gift; there's no Sears and Roebuck, although you would probably find a few Smith and Wesson's. But there are surprises; a half block away, an old panel truck stood parked next to a small frame building; on its sides, in red letters, appeared: IN THE NAME OF JESUS TIRE COMPANY. All of the tires were flat. As I waited to turn left onto Twenty Fourth Street, I saw him, all overalls, white hair and beard. His skin was as black as his beard was white, and his right hand melted into a cane, but he seemed uncertain how to use it. The traffic noise, the crowded street, seemed to confuse him. As I turned the corner, I saw him step down from the curb, then retreat to the safety of the sidewalk. I pulled to a stop a half block away, and walked back to the corner. As the light changed, I offered him my arm, and we safely crossed the street. Safe on the sidewalk, he reached down into his long, right pocket, down into another century, took my right hand and deposited a single blue marble in the palm of my hand. No words, only the single marble. As he disappeared down the street. I held the marble up to the sun, and saw a man with a dark beard, under white stars and deep, green foliage; the cane is now a flute, and as he plays, I hear voices in a vowel-dominated language surrounding him. I do not know what it means, Alphie, but so much for flat tires, and a lousy place to find a gift.

The World

I thought of calling this La Belle Dame Sans Merci—the Beautiful, Merciless Lady—because she certainly was. I was in the third grade of a rural Ohio, one-room school. She was in the eighth grade, and I know what you are thinking. But it's just that one day as I watched her across the room, avoiding her dark brown eyes, she flipped her jet black tresses across her neck, and somehow, my heart got tangled in the dark strands of her hair. I was a totally secretive lover, at least until one day, when I passed her while she spoke with her friends during recess. I learned that her birthday was approaching, in April, near mine. I would find the perfect gift, and she would wait for me to grow up. The next weekend in downtown Hamilton, I found "The Gift." I would give her the world. Actually, it was a small globe, mostly blue, with the countries in yellow. It really was a pencil sharpener, and if you inserted the pencil between Borneo and New Zealand, twisted the pencil a few times, you had a sharpened pencil. I bought the deluxe model, which came with a new pencil, wrapped it in blue paper, and on her birthday, before class, handed it to her, and wished her happy birthday, hoping she couldn't hear my bass drum heart beating. She made no response, and at the end of the school day, I bolted from the room, and headed home without looking back, not wanting to become a pillar of salt. The next day I began to worry, since she hadn't even spoken to me. At recess, I had to pass a group of girls; she seemed to be the center of attention of the group. Then I heard her voice. She was actually speaking to me. If you can call one word "speaking." "Jack," she said, and held up the globe for everyone to see; then she inserted a pencil and began moving it in and out, in and out, rapidly, geographical intercourse, for all to see. I think a part of me died there, globally speaking. But I did learn something. I still think it was a great gift; but if you have any expectations about the giving of a gift---fuhgeddaboudit!

Sex

It is morning recess at a rural school in southern Ohio. My friend, Jimmy, is absent, so I seek a corner of the grassy playground, next to a small ditch, behind a tool shed. I find my so-called lunch, a peanut butter sandwich, which I hate, and throw it over the fence to join dozens of others I had rejected. I am lying on my back, looking at clouds shaped like animals, when Janet, a second grader, sits down beside me. We have hardly spoken, but as I raise my arm to point out a lion-cloud, she suddenly rolls over on top of me and kisses me, right on the lips. In the midst of trying to cope with this new experience, I have the sensation of warmth around my stomach. Then awareness is on the attack; I have peed in my pants. Janet jumps to her feet, with a cry of disgust, and disappears around the tool shed. We never mentioned the incident in our future brief encounters. I sometimes wondered if her sexual development might have been delayed by the experience.

I know there is a hose on the other side of the shed, so I rinse myself off, pleased that no one seemed to have noticed anything. I walk briskly to the classroom entrance, and am the first one into the room. I hurry to my desk, open my oversized geography book, and place it over my legs. I wonder if, the following year, when a student opens the book to pages 72 and 73—the Ukraine: Breadbasket of the East—he might ponder the crinkled pages. He will probably think it was rain. Better that he never know.

Lies, Truth, and Communication

Myth Maker

Before I understood the concept of myth—some say myth is somebody else's religion—I created my own myths, and took part in them. When I was walking down a certain street, feeling bored, I would say, "If I don't reach that oak tree up ahead, before that oncoming car, may God strike me dead." Actually, I was quite careful to allow myself plenty of time to reach the tree first, sometimes cutting it a little close, to make it interesting. It always gave me a lift, cheating death right there on Elm Street in Hamilton, Ohio, on an otherwise uninteresting Saturday morning. Naturally, one day it happened. I tripped on a wide crack in the sidewalk, fell forward, and watched helplessly as the blue Dodge zipped by. I folded myself into a fetal position, tears running down my cheeks, and at that point a kindly woman bent over me, and asked: "What's the matter?" So what do I tell her? That I am lying there moaning because a car beat me to a tree? Do I want to be in the Insane Asylum by nightfall? I pointed to my scraped, bloody knee, and she gave me a handkerchief, and a pat on the head. And, temporarily, I became an ex-myth maker. I also assumed that God had taken out a large, black notebook, and, after moistening the tip of the pencil between His lips, under the heading, LIES, made the appropriate notation.

The Leaf

On the first of a dozen trips to Spain, while attending Summer School in Segovia, there was the aqueduct, the Alcazar, the storks on the bell tower, and Pilar. We met at a meeting of students who were fans of the Spanish poet, Antonio Machado. There were readings of Machado's work, discussions, and sometimes slides. We became accustomed to staying afterward, sharing a glass of vino tinto and our favorite poems of Machado. When Summer School ended, we met for the last time, to say goodbye, early morning in October, near the railroad station. As we spoke, there seemed to be an emphasis on our seeing each other in the future. I wouldn't have thought that we would lie to each other, but the lies just kept piling up, like autumn leaves under a Sycamore tree. "You'll be coming back to Spain soon," she observed, "and I might come to America." Each affirmation led to a more implausible affirmation, as the lies piled up. At that moment, a cold gust of the October wind, disguised as November, dragged a dry leaf across the cobblestoned street. No more words, only the truth of the dry leaf, reflected in the other's eyes. We each turned, and walked away. I think that's one of the things that Antonio Machado's poetry is about. And we had shared another of his verses.

Communication

Among the social events of the Trenton Presbyterian Church, shades of Jon Benet, was the annual Tom Thumb Wedding, in which two children, six to eight years old, were "married" in the Main Hall of the church. No, I was not the groom; I was an eight-year-old minister, having the reputation of being able to memorize material easily. It really was a fun experience for me, up to a point. I had no trouble memorizing the ritual, and enjoyed the dark suit, complete with a stiff, white collar, that I wore. Perhaps I enjoyed it too much. All those adults looking down at me, shaking my hand, saying things like, "Great service, Reverend Jack." By the time we had finished the lemonade and cookies, and taken the drive home, I had become rather accustomed to my celebrity status. It had even occurred to me to sleep in my suit. I guess you could say that the whole ritual had gone, not to my head, but to my neck, or perhaps to the collar that seemed to be the seat of power. Possessed by this new-found power, I boldly walked into the kitchen, where my mother was preparing a pot of coffee. "You had better be good to me," I said, wagging a finger at her, as I had seen Shirley Temple do on many occasions, "or I am going to tell God on you." I remember a certain confusion, as I looked into my mother's eyes; one eye seemed to show amusement, the other, annoyance. It seemed a long time, before she said anything—almost as long as Sunday Service in the Trenton Presbyterian Church. Then she said, in a very low voice, "So you have a direct line of communication with God." "Yes I do," I replied. "Well," she said, as her right hand swooped down on my collar, like a barn owl swooping down on a field mouse, "You have just been ex-communicated." So much for the short, happy life of Reverend Jack.

The Look

There was a sadness about my mother, as I perceived her, the sadness of a broken swing, empty, among a row of swings filled with children. Her left leg, decimated by Infantile Paralysis as a teenager, left her with a pronounced limp. I never heard her complain, not even when, during Ohio winters, the green pain invaded her leg. When I walked with her, I usually felt like a guard; I hated the people who made clucking sounds as they passed us, when she smoked on the street. And I hated even more the young boys who would mimic her walk, prancing around behind us. And, about the men she attracted, you could say, "She certainly deserved better!"

They tended to be S men—shady, smooth, suspicious, sexist, and I suppose, sexy, best represented by the slimy insurance salesman, who was a too-frequent visitor. One day, I encountered him at the top of the stairs, and he touched my shoulder and asked—with only the suggestion of a smirk, "Hey kid, your mother home? I'm sure she is." And he touched my shirt, above my ribs, with his elbow. Decades later, I would laugh, but with an accompanying bitterness, at a Monty Python routine: "So your wife likes to go on vacations without you? Bet she does, bet she does, nudge, nudge!"

But my mother had her strengths. Among them was, what I called, The Look. When she needed to control me, she was able to isolate all the energy within her, and concentrate it in her eyes. While in this state, nothing seemed to exist except her eyes, and my quivering self. Darth Vader would have traded his laser wand for The Look any day. I usually knew when I was guilty of some unacceptable act. Words were my only defense. I would spend hours working on a detailed series of phrases that would, hopefully, convince her of my innocence. But, sometimes, she would respond with The Look, halfway through my carefully thought out verbal essay. And before you could say "Man overboard!" consonants and vowels were clinging to life rafts, their gibberish-like screams drowned out by the crashing waves. And that led to The Sunday.

That day, my mother, my step father, and I visited the Allisons—perhaps the only affluent family we knew—on a remote farm in southern Ohio. I was nine, and on arriving, I sought the Allison's teenage son, Henry, found him behind the corn crib, smoking a Camel cigarette. He immediately grasped me by my shirt front, bully that he was, and mentioned several violent possibilities that might result, if I should communicate with his parents regarding his smoking. Later, when we were playing croquet (how elegant!) on the beautiful, emerald green front lawn, I had a chance to knock his ball away; for some reason, I felt immune to his threats, and the sound of my mallet striking his ball was among those beautiful sounds that one remembers for a long, long time. His ball went flying off the lawn, into the corn field, and we never did find it. Henry left in his hot rod, the spinning wheels communicating his anger. Perhaps buoyed by this success, I skipped into the house, to see what other surprises awaited me. I would not be disappointed.

We had had a salad for lunch, but were not staying for dinner. I was sitting at the kitchen table, reading the comics, when Mrs. Allison entered, and asked if I was hungry. Before I could answer, she opened a cupboard door and asked, "Would you like a bowl of Rice Krispies?" What a question! We didn't even have a place for Rice Krispies in our kitchen, but I had a master list, in my head, of families whose cupboards contained Rice Krispies. And, believe me, it was a short list! Our breakfast was always the same: oat meal with hot water, and usually, no sugar. Rice Krispies! Only strawberry ice cream rated higher with me, and add a banana to the Rice Krispies, and it was number one. As I observed the beauty of the bright red and white box, a shadow fell over the table, and me, and the box of Rice Krispies; my mother was framed in the doorway, her face obviously in its pre-Look phase. It was then that I heard a voice, not recognizable as mine, saying what I must not say, "Why yes, Mrs. Allison, that would be great!" And I'm still alive! And it will have to be one of those unsolved mysteries. Part of me is still convinced that The Look will take the three parts of the Y and form them into an N, and then complete the change to a negative response. But it doesn't happen. And I am aware that the doorway is, now, amazingly, empty. But now, I am too fascinated watching Mrs. Allison slice half a banana into full moons on the Rice Krispies, pour on some cream, and then slide a bowl of sugar across the table. Responding to my disappearing act with the bowl of cereal, she offers me (There is a God!) a second. Do you think I refuse?

The first few minutes of the drive home were tense, to say the least. In the pitch darkness of the car, the brightness of the car's instrument panel was matched only by the sound of my beating heart. When will it come? I ask myself. It never did. I fell asleep in the back seat, and dreamed cereal dreams. But what dreams!

Somehow the emerald green of the lawn had evoked a kind of Ozian magic. In the dream, I walk in from the black and white corn field, to the dazzling emerald lawn, the brightly purple, red, blue, green croquet balls, the red and white two-feet-tall box of Rice Krispies sitting on the porch, and begin to play croquet. But what a difference! Now I am playing with Snap, Crackle, and Pop; Snap and I are partners, as are Crackle and Pop. And the game is very different; we help each other to get through the wickets. And when one makes a good shot, we all drop our mallets and dance around the wickets.

I don't know if they ever found the croquet ball in the cornfield. Maybe it's still there. I think a part of me still is.

The Party

The week before my seventh birthday, I defined the verbs "to beg," and "to grovel." I wanted to have a birthday party, just a small one; I had decided that six guests from school, and me, would make a magic combination of seven celebrating seven. My mother informed me that this "seven argument" was the weakest part of my case, but that, anyway, there just wasn't enough money. Her argument was as deadly as the "you'll shoot your eye out" argument was for a boy wanting a BB gun.

The morning of my birthday started just like any other day; then it took a strange turn. This is a disclaimer: don't ask me to explain some of my actions that morning. I'm sure part of me must have stepped out of my body to say, "Are you crazy?" At recess, I gathered the six selected guests near the fence, and told them that they needed to inform their parents that they were invited to a birthday party at my house, right after school. I even suggested that they not communicate this to any of the other students, and that my mother would take them home after the party.

And that explains this group of seven, walking between wheat fields, walking the mile of paved highway, smelling the tar, partially melted in the warm sun; I was the Pied Piper of Ice Cream and Cake, leading them to the Birthday Party That Wasn't. When we arrived at the farm where I lived, I led them directly to the kitchen. "What have we here?" asked my mother. It should be noted here that, at this moment, clocks reportedly stopped throughout the Western World, and maybe even the Eastern. If the Guinness Book of Records had existed then, the next minute would have been the longest in history. "They're here for my birthday party," I replied. The next minute was the second longest in history. "Well, then," she said, "I guess I better drive to the store and get some ice cream and cake." If I had had a direct line to God, at that moment, she would have been sainted on the spot.

The next hour was spent showing them the animals, and one of the farm hands gave them a ride on the John Deere tractor. When it started to rain, we headed for the barn, where we climbed stacked bales of hay, which offered a jumping off place into a giant stack of straw. When we tired of this, and with the downpour becoming heavier, we all climbed to the top of the stacks of baled hay. We found a place where we could all lie, next to a wide door that opened outward, toward the rain, about twenty feet above the ground. There was something about the heavy rain, only a few inches away, that seemed to, at the same time, bring us closer to each other, and isolate us from the adult world. Perhaps it was the heavenly aroma of the hay mixed with that of the rain. Each of us had acquired a piece of straw, which alternately hung from the mouth, sometimes bobbing up and down when we spoke, and sometimes was removed to emphasize certain words. Surely we were, for a while, worldly adults with the required cigarette necessary for the fascinating conversations we had seen in the movies. During the next hour, we talked about our lives more openly than usual, our successes, and our failures.

When the rain stopped, we headed for the house, and strawberry ice cream and sponge cake. No paper hats, no Pin the Tail on the Donkey, no balloons. But, as darkness approached, and my mother herded them toward the car, I felt it had been a great party, perhaps the best I ever attended. Loading the small Chevrolet was a combination of my mother's exasperated shouts and the giggles of the six children. Finally, shouted "Happy Birthdays" as the car pulled on to the road, and turned right. I walked out to the road and followed the bright red tail light, until it disappeared in the darkness. Then I skipped up the sidewalk, climbed the stairs two at a time to my bedroom, and leaped on the bed. It had been a long day, but a great day. She spoke and there were no words, she sang and there were no songs. There was a birthday party where there was no birthday party. I still think that watching that tail light in the darkness was one of the happiest moments of my life. I have learned to remember it, and using a tiny VCR in my head, I watch the tail light disappear, let the lightning bugs out of the Mason jar, put it on Rewind and relive the whole afternoon. It's a great way to fall asleep.

American Flyer

Cozy, but with an occasional shiver. That's how it was on this late spring afternoon in Cincinnati; I was eight, and a light but steady rain was falling on the recently cut grass of the front lawn, and on a red wagon on the sidewalk. On the side of the wagon was AMERICAN FLYER, in red letters, with white wings on each side of the letters. The rain did not touch me, for I was on a wooden swing, at the end of a covered porch, and from time to time I would breathe in the scent of the rain-grass, amazed at how it made me feel. Andrew Weil would have been proud of me. I was not alone. Seated in a wicker chair was a woman shelling peas into a round metal bowl. Carrie was her name and grandmother was her game. For some, she was defined by her size; arms like peninsulas, she could barely squeeze into the largest of chairs. From time to time, she would look up and smile, a warm-blanket-with-a-purring-kitten-by-the-fire smile that sent a kind of cosmic message that only we understood. Now, as the swing begins its upward arc, I leap forward, and run to the wicker chair, to lie across the shelled peas, my face buried in one of her massive arms. Now the grass-rain aroma is joined by cinnamon and green apples, and I know that along with a regular size apple pie, the oven also contains a small pie, with a large J in the center. I don't think I ever really understood what we had in common, my grandmother and I—nor was it necessary to understand. But now, looking back, I think it was, among other things, judgment by physical characteristics. We were Laurel and Hardy. In my case it was the S word; the nurse at school, all those students in line for a physical, she has to say: "My, you're a skinny one!" And then the laughter when she reads the number from the tape measure around my chest. With my grandmother, the nurse was replaced by my grandfather—although the truth is, I believe that I thought of him as being more like the anti-grandfather. It is a family gathering, my grandmother has worked in the kitchen all day. I sit on a high stool, helping her when I can. She sits down in the living room for only a few minutes, and my grandfather says, to all the dozen people assembled, "Well, if we can find a crane big enough to lift Carrie out of that chair, we can all come to dinner." I head for the bathroom to wipe away the hot tears, and I think of my own grandfather as I think of the bully kicking sand in the face of the 98-pound weakling in the Charles Atlas ads. On one occasion, my mother told me that she would prefer that I call my grandmother, Carrie, since she was not really my grandmother, that my grandfather had remarried after the death of my mother's mother, and that we were not even related to her. "Blood is thicker than water," she reminded me. I wish I could have known enough to remind her that water can run very deep.

And this day, it certainly ran deep. The rain drops striking the red wagon and the peas striking the metal bowl formed the point-counterpoint of a kind of aromatic melody, combining the cut grass, the rain, cinnamon, and green apples. Feeling like a graduate of the Charles Atlas Academy, I propel the swing higher and higher, and in a kind of Oz-ian phenomenon, perhaps aided by the wings on the red wagon, the porch, the swing, the wicker chair, the bowl of peas, the red wagon, the rain, and Carrie and me, all climb up, up, up—above fatness and skinniness, above meanness and tape measures and scales—where only love and joy exist.

And for a few moments—forever—I was, truly, a veritable American Flyer.

The Morning

One day in June, on the farm in southern Ohio, I awakened just after dawn, and as was my habit, with my knees on the bed, my elbows on the sill of the open window, I observed, with affection, the morning. On one of the swaying top branches, a robin proclaimed the beauty of the lilac bush, in full bloom. The sun had just now touched the single pear of my favorite tree, and in a hollow part of its trunk was a small cigar box filled with my treasures, shiny rocks, a piece of a Robin's egg, a coin from Mexico. The grass had been cut the previous evening, and as I inhaled that aroma, something happened that, at first, I thought I might have caused. But it was a sudden breeze that moved the single, white curtain to my left, moved it so that it touched my left cheek. And, somehow, thanks to the white curtain, I was no longer someone observing the beauty of the universe, I was a part of that universe. The same aliveness that was in the lilac bush's blooms, and the robin's song, was in me. Being alive at this precise moment was a miracle of miracles. Years later, I would recognize the structure of the experience in the concept of "synecdoche," the part for the whole, "to see the world in a grain of sand." But no rational explanation could come close to the experience. At the same time, we seem to have a need to explain our experiences rationally. As I skipped into the kitchen that June morning, my mother commented on my entrance: "Who wound you up this morning?" I just couldn't tell her that a curtain touched my cheek, so I came up with "I found a nickel under the bed." Many years later, in graduate school in Oregon, I would encounter a poem by Juan Ramon Jimenez, in which he describes the movement of a curtain as representing the entire life-giving power of the Universe. That I shared such an experience with a man from another culture, another language, seemed almost as miraculous as the experience itself.

A few years ago, on a late afternoon in Sedona, I am sitting in a booth in a restaurant, and a sudden breeze moves a curtain in the open window, and a sense of the joy of life surges through me once more. Then I hear, in the background, one of Joni Mitchell's songs, about Kansas, and Dorothy is "standing by the window, looking for another windy day." Me too, Joni. Me too.

Printed in the United States
By Bookmasters